D1569964

Blake and the New Age

Blake and the New Age

KATHLEEN RAINE

London
GEORGE ALLEN & UNWIN
Boston   Sydney

GEORGE ALLEN & UNWIN LTD
40 Museum Street, London WC1A 1LU

© George Allen & Unwin (Publishers) Ltd, 1979

British Library Cataloguing in Publication Data

Raine, Kathleen
    Blake and the new age.
    1. Blake, William – Criticism and interpretation
    I. Title
    821'.7   PR4147   79–40013

    ISBN 0–04–821043–9

Typeset in 11 on 12 point Plantin by Trade Linotype Ltd, Birmingham
and printed in Great Britain
by William Clowes, Beccles and London

Foreword

These chapters, written for various occasions and over a number of years since the publication of my *Blake and Tradition*, have a common theme. All are studies of Blake's thought as it has an immediate bearing on changes taking place at the present time. The end of the nineteenth century and the first half of our own may well be seen, in the future, not as the time of some final triumph of the materialist world-order, but as the beginning of a reversal of the premises upon which that world-order is constructed. It is no more possible to find absolute beginnings than it is to find the source of a river; at most one can point to a trickle in a certain direction, which presently gathers tributary trickles, until we can say that there is a stream. Such I believe is the present situation: there are many indications that mind, not matter, is once again being considered as the first principle of the universe in which we find ourselves but of which we can know so little. Of this reversal of premises the Romantic poets – especially Coleridge and Blake – were forerunners. Blake was the first to speak of a 'New Age' in this sense; whose advent his greatest follower, W. B. Yeats was to reaffirm, and whose tide is now flowing in a generation moved by forces on a collective scale. And what else is a New Age but a change of premises?

Blake's prophetic message was to his own nation, England, the Giant Albion; and in a lesser degree to other Western nations, France and America in particular. He called himself a 'prophet', in the tradition of the Old Testament prophets whose words were directed to their nation and concerned national life. Blake, unread and misunderstood in his own lifetime, seems to many to speak especially to the present generation. We now begin to possess the knowledge – especially of the archetypal structure of the human psyche – which enables us to comprehend many things he wrote which were incomprehensible at the turn of the eighteenth century. He believed himself to be inspired; by what in earlier ages would have been called a God, or the Holy Spirit. Now that inspiring genius has other names – Yeats's *anima mundi*, C. G. Jung's 'Collective Unconscious' or transpersonal Self. But by whatever name, the communications of that 'other' mind are of an order beyond any personal construction or fantasy; they concern us all, for they are spoken by the Imagination to the imagination. Blake knew that he was the messenger to his nation from the higher and inner worlds; and he took upon himself to deliver that message to deaf ears, to obdurate opinion, to indifference. In symbolic narrative, in pictorial image, in rational argument and in the exaltation of poetry he strove to awaken the national consciousness to the vision he himself so clearly beheld.

It is for those readers who see in Blake an inspired teacher, but who are perhaps greatly bewildered when they attempt to discover what it was that he taught, that this book is intended.

It is not a work for the academic, but for the common reader, and especially for those in search of what Blake himself claims to have possessed, spiritual knowledge.

Several of these essays have been given as lectures on different occasions and to audiences of widely different kinds; *Thomas Taylor and the English Romantic Movement* at Royaumont (Colloques Internationaux du Centre National de la Recherche Scientifique) in 1969. *Blake and Wordsworth* was written for the Cheltenham Festival of Literature (1972). *Berkeley, Blake and the New Age* was the Berkeley Lecture at Trinity College, Dublin in 1975; *Everything that Lives is Holy* the Beard Memorial Lecture (1978) at the College of Psychic Studies (London). *Innocence and Experience* is a paper given to the Meher Baba Society (London) in 1977.

Blake's Christianity was one of a series of lectures arranged by the Theological School at King's College, London (1976). An earlier and shorter version of *Blake's Last Judgment* was published by the Ampleforth Review.

Berkeley, Blake and the New Age was published as a pamphlet in 1977 by the Golgonooza Press. I wish to thank Mr. Brian Keeble for agreeing to the inclusion of this essay in the present collection; and all those Societies and Institutions named above for having provided the occasions for setting in order some of my thoughts on Blake.

Page references to the Oxford Standard Edition of the writings of Blake, edited by Geoffrey Keynes are indicated by 'K' followed by the page number.

KATHLEEN RAINE
London, May 1978

Contents

I *England's Prophet*

William Blake might almost be called a poet of the twentieth century; for it was not until 1927 that Geoffrey Keynes's None-such edition made his complete writings available to the nation for whom he wrote. Blake has been called a mystic; a word which suggests an other-wordly contemplative. But Blake's genius was not of that kind. He called himself a prophet; Blake was England's single prophet, 'one who speaks for God', addressing himself to the English nation on matters of public concern.

In 1927 Blake was a still relatively unknown poet with a reputation for obscurity and eccentricity, shadowed by rumours of madness. The rumours are unfounded – Blake's only mental abnormality was an altogether exceptional degree of sanity. But so strange did Blake's ideas seem to the nineteenth century, so incomprehensible his unknown mythology, that the imputation is not surprising. Yet so great was the respect Blake had inspired among his contemporaries, so deep the devotion of those who called his poor dwelling 'the House of the Interpreter', that he yet remained a radiant figure throughout a century in which his written works were unprinted and his best paintings mouldered in attics. His young disciples remembered that to walk with him was 'like walking with the Prophet Isaiah'.

When Alexander Gilchrist was writing his life of Blake (completed after his death by William Michael Rossetti and published in 1893) he was still able to draw upon the memories of Samuel Palmer, Calvert, George Richmond and others still living who remembered Blake. These testified to the simple majesty of the old engraver who had been the master and the inspiration of the young painters who called themselves 'the Shoreham Ancients'. Samuel Palmer, writing in 1885 to Gilchrist, recalls Blake as he recollected him nearly thirty years after his death:

> In him you saw at once the Maker, the Inventor; one of the few in any age: a fitting companion for Dante. He was

energy itself, and shed around him a kindling influence; and atmosphere of life, full of the ideal . . . He was a man without a mask; his aim was single, his path straightforwards, and his wants few; so he was free, noble and happy . . . His eye was the finest I ever saw: brilliant, but not roving, clear and intent, yet susceptible; it flashed with genius, or melted in tenderness. It could also be terrible. Cunning and falsehood quailed under it, but it was never busy with them. It pierced them and turned away . . .

Such was Blake as I remember him. He was one of the few to be met with in our passage through life, who are not, in some way or other, 'double-minded' and inconsistent with themselves; one of the very few who cannot be depressed by neglect, and to whose name rank and station could add no lustre . . . He ennobled poverty, and, by his conversation and the influence of his genius, made two small rooms in Fountain Court more attractive than the threshold of princes.

Even now any reader who plunges unprepared into *Milton* or *Jerusalem* will share the bewilderment of earlier generations, for these obscure English poems offer no narrative clue or sequential argument, no familiar earthly landscape, no identifiable characters of this, or any other world. If some names are familiar (Milton's, for example) it is as if we were to meet a person of that name in a bewildering dream. If we read on it is for the joy of some sudden illumination, some radiant fragment of heavenly vision, or earthly common sense which shatters hypocrisy and shocks and shakes us into amazed admiration. But these sudden illuminations are in a context, a matrix as turbulent as Lear's 'vexed sea'; as Yeats wrote,

The surface is perpetually, as it were, giving way before one, and revealing another surface below it, and that again dissolves when we try to study it. The making of religion melts into the making of the earth, and that fades away into some allegory of the rising and the setting of the sun. It is all like a great cloud full of stars and shapes through which the eye seeks a boundary in vain. When we seemed to have explored the remotest division some new spirit floats by muttering wisdom.

(*Blake's Prophetic Books* Ellis & Yeats, Vol. I p. 287)

Yeats gave a clue to Blake's Prophecies in suggesting that these unexplained transformations follow the Swedenborgian law of 'correspondence', in accordance with which scenes and the whole aspect of things, changes with our thoughts, as indeed happens continuously in dreams. But Blake is not describing dreams; rather a state of clearer knowledge he called 'vision'. Plato, he said 'has made Socrates say that Poets & Prophets do not know or Understand what they write or Utter; this is a most Pernicious Falsehood. If they do not, pray is an inferior kind to be call'd Knowing?' (K. 605)

He himself was in no doubt as to the value of what he had to impart. He makes a clear promise to his readers so simple and so immense that we do believe him, notwithstanding our own incomprehension,

> I give you the end of a golden string,
> Only wind it into a ball,
> It will lead you in at Heaven's Gate
> Built in Jerusalem's wall.
>
> (K. 551)

That clue leads us on and on, from the simple beginnings of *Songs of Innocence and Experience*; we wind our way through the relatively easy *Book of Thel* and *Visions of the Daughters of Albion* into the great labyrinth of *Jerusalem*. Those who persist are not disappointed: Blake keeps his word. The threading of his maze has the value of an initiation, a transformation of consciousness, exhilarating and liberating. It is not the world that is changed but ourselves; we see with new eyes.

The only book of Blake's which during his lifetime found any publisher but himself was his charming collection of *juvenilia*, *Poetical Sketches*. *The French Revolution* reached the proof stage; but even his radical friend Johnson the bookseller and publisher of St Paul's Churchyard did not dare, in the end, to issue this now unreadable work. No great loss: for although as a young man Blake had Jacobin sympathies his was not to be a political revolution, but, far more radical, a spiritual apokatastasis.

It is true that *Songs of Innocence and Experience* were republished several times during the nineteenth century. In Gilchrist's *Life of William Blake* long passages from the Prophetic Books were printed; but not until 1887 (in a limited and costly edition) were the whole of the Prophetic Books first published; imperfectly edited by Edwin J. Ellis and W. B. Yeats. Only then did Blake begin to be known for the giant he was. Readers expecting to find a naive mystic of almost child-like simplicity were daunted by those 'stupendous works,' products of a volcanic imagination welded by the force of powerful intellectual energy. Swinburne, doubtless delighted by Blake's advocacy of 'free love,' and taking literally his announcement of the 'Bible of Hell', acclaimed our national prophet as the poet of 'Evil'. The Decadents, the Surréalists, the Marxists, have all in turn laid claim to him, but he is not to be contained in any of their smaller measures.

The editorial and bibliographical labours of Sir Geoffrey Keynes over the last half century have made Blake accessible, but not comprehensible. Now however a whole body of knowledge necessary to the understanding of Blake has begun to be uncovered in the records of the past, or discovered in fields of study altogether new. Blake, laboriously engraving and illuminating the few copies of his marvellous books for which he was able to find purchasers, was a hundred years in advance of his time. Yet he had the assurance of a knowledge which he almost alone then possessed, that a time would come when he would be understood. To the future he addressed himself in his preface to *Milton: A Prophecy*:

> Rouze up, O Young Men of the New Age! Set your fore-
> heads against the ignorant Hirelings! For we have Hirelings
> in the Camp, the Court & the University, who would, if they
> could, for ever depress Mental, & prolong Corporeal War.
> Painters! on you I call. Sculptors! Architects!   (K. 480)

Such a challenge issued in a work which did not find one purchaser might seem pathetic, indeed tragic, were it not for the vindication of Blake's faith in the fulness of time. It is the young men of the 'Age of Aquarius' who chalk on the walls of Blake's native London, 'The tygers of wrath are wiser than the horses of instruction' and other aphorisms from the *Marriage of Heaven and Hell*. If fifty years ago the problem of an editor was to vindicate a neglected poet, the mystery now to be explained is why Blake's works should take their place among the sacred books of a 'new age'. It is doubtful whether the writers of slogans understand Blake any better than his first readers, or have read beyond the *Marriage of Heaven and Hell* whence their revolutionary aphorisms are mined. But their instinctive recognition that Blake's teaching is for their new 'Age of Aquarius' would be deepened and confirmed were they to do so, although their ideas about the character of that age might be much changed in the process. Blake did loose a Tyger on the world, and in Aleister Crowley's words 'the beast that broke through the mazes of heaven was so vast that its claws spanned star and star.'

Blake was indeed the first poet to speak of a New Age. That Age was neither his own nor that of the revolutions of his time (in which however he certainly read the signs of its advent) but the fulfilment of the prophecy of Emanuel Swedenborg; who had even given a date – 1757 – for its advent in 'the heavens' (by which he meant the inner worlds of the mind.) Blake was born in that year, and this doubtless added to his sense of being a chosen instrument for the fulfilment of his teacher's prophecy.

I do not remember that before the Second World War, or for many years after it, writers or artists ever spoke of a new age. True, T. S. Eliot and others of his generation spoke of the end of European civilization and the advent of a new 'dark age'. Those in whom Eliot might have seen portents of that coming darkness wished to be (in Rimbaud's words) *'absolument moderne'*; Herbert Read was the spokesman of the 'modern movement' and 'modern art'. Some, like the Surréalists, declared themselves 'revolutionary,' or even, in the political sense, *'au service de la révolution'*. But this avant-gardism was quite another thing from the proclamation of the mutation of an age. That proclamation came, paradoxically enough, from Yeats who was looked upon by the moderns of his day as 'reactionary' because he did not write 'free verse' or subscribe to Marxist politics.

But Yeats had understood that Blake's new age was something more radical than the innovation of a new style in art. What both these poets foresaw was indeed the end of that European Christendom of which Eliot is perhaps the last great English-speaking poet, and the advent of an epoch not to be (as the evolutionists suppose) a farther development of existing knowledge but a reversal of values, a change in the premises of knowledge itself. Blake's Tygers of Wrath foreshadow Yeats's:

And what rough beast, its hour come round at last
Slouches towards Bethlehem to be born?
                              (The Second Coming)

This reversal might be seen less as a revolution than as a restoration; and it is interesting to note that two earlier movements owing much to Blake had named themselves 'the Shoreham Ancients,' and the 'Pre-Raphaelites'. Both names indicating rather a wish to restore, to rediscover lost knowledge, than to follow existing 'progressive' trends.

Yeats's own Prophetic Book, *A Vision* (first published, in an edition of only six hundred copies, in the same year as Keynes's Nonsuch edition of Blake – 1927) describes history in terms of a diagram in the form of triangles (or cones) each with its apex touching the other's base; between the two poles the cycle of the years for ever turns in 'gyres.' This idea was known to antiquity. Plato in the *Laws* speaks of the reversal of the revolutions of the world which takes place as Golden Age and Iron Age succeed one another in perpetual alternation. He too uses the idea of gyrations, describing the world as either guided in its revolutions by God, or left to itself, to run down like a spring released, by its own momentum.

The precession of the equinox was known to Egypt and Babylon; and it was universally believed, in antiquity, that a new age was announced at the transition of the equinox from one sign of the zodiac to the next; an event which occurs approximately every two thousand years. Virgil was held by the early Church to be a prophet of Christ because in the Fourth Eclogue he writes of the advent of a Golden Age. The Apocalypse of St John announces the same event as a 'new heaven and new earth'. Doubtless both authors were familiar with the supposed mutation of an age at the beginning of the Great Year which began when the equinox moved from Aries to Pisces. Yeats, himself an astrologer, was familiar with this tradition and to him the advent of the 'Age of Aquárius' when the equinox leaves Pisces, was well known. But within the Judeaeo–Christian tradition, time is conceived as linear, and the world as having a beginning and an end; a view not shared (or shared only with misgivings) by Blake, who speaks of the 'endless circle' of the time-world, therefore whereas both Swedenborg (in his concept of 'Churches') and Boehme saw the successive ages as leading to the Christian Millennium at the end of time, Blake in several passages in the Prophetic Books gives evidence of Plato's influence on his thought in this matter. Does the cycle, having reached its end, begin again? Blake, in sympathy with the American and French Revolutions (at least as a young man) viewed the immediate changes with optimism, no doubt strengthened by his belief, as a Swedenborgian, that the age about to begin – the 'church' of the 'Divine Human' – was to bring mankind nearer the millennium. But later, when he wrote that strange poem *The Mental Traveller* he seems to have come nearer to Plato's view. This poem – one of the principle sources of Yeats's *A Vision* – is a mythical narrative expressing the idea to which Yeats gave diagrammatic form in his gyres, of the continual movement between two opposite principles, each, as it were, growing at the other's expense.

Why (whether or not their time be marked on the clock-face of the heavens) do such changes come about? Swedenborg (who was by profession a scientist) may have been near the truth in his view that everything in this world, whether a living organism, a 'church' or a civilization, begins with a spiritual impulse and ends in a fixed form; the form complete, the force is spent. This is a law of nature; and when some civilization has expressed fully the possibilities inherent in the impulse from which it originated, it must, however great its achievement, come to its end. Every effort to 'save civilization' must be as futile as to prolong life beyond its natural span. Political preferences do not matter; and as Blake's optimism was tempered by the knowledge that every new impulse will in time be spent, so Yeats's pessimism about the immediate future was tempered by the knowledge that 'gyres run on' and all that seems lost will return.

Blake saw the Messiah of the new age as the 'frowning Babe,' whom he called Orc. He is the hairy Esau, Yeats's 'rough beast.' Orc, with his 'fiery limbs and flaming hair,' 'the new-born terror,' 'the son of fire in his eastern cloud,' dominates *The Marriage of Heaven and Hell* and the earlier Prophetic Books. Orc is, like the Tyger, a symbol of 'evil, or energy,' as opposed to the 'good' of 'reason'; and of Blake's exultation in the new birth and the impending overthrow of all the senile institutions of the old order, there can be no doubt.

Blake's 'good' and 'evil' are not, of course, in themselves good or evil in an absolute sense; they are the 'contraries' without which there is 'no progression'; for with a new age comes a reversal of values. Blake, who undertook to write 'the Bible of Hell' declares that what reason calls evil – irrational energy, the spirit of prophecy, and 'the grandeur of Inspiration' – is to be the law of the new age. The 'Messiah, or Reason' of the old order (not to be confused with Blake's 'Jesus, the Imagination' who 'was all virtue, and acted from impulse, not from rules') was the governor of the unwilling.

Reason calls the irrational energies 'evil'. Conversely, the supreme figure of Reason becomes for the new-born spirit of Orc, 'Aged Ignorance' who clips the wings of life. The claims to of the blind rational faculty to be 'God', the figures so memorably depicted as aged Urizen, have imposed a tyranny both moral and intellectual. Blake attacked at once the cold Deism of a rationalised religion and the new Goddess Reason of the Enlightenment. He saw in the various revolutionary movements of his youth the protest of life, ignorant, joyous and ever-young, against the systems and institutions of a civilization dominated by rational deductions from the evidence of the five senses; held, by Locke and others whom Blake attacks, to be the only sources of knowledge.

By the younger generation of the 'Age of Aquarius' Blake is seen as a figure of power because he first manifested the reversal of an archetypal situation. For these young people of the 'New Age' the symbolic figure of 'Old Nobodaddy', the paternal figure of (to borrow a term from Jung) the 'wise old man,' has been replaced by the *puer eternus*, the Divine Child, the life-principle, not the reason. 'Life delights in life', Blake said; words which express the best in the new spirit of a generation for whom the holy is indeed a reality; but not in the guise of old forms and institutions of churches, not in the 'man of sorrows' but in Shiva Nataraja, 'Lord of the dance'. These find all they need of Blake in the figure of Orc, new-born to overthrow the aged tyrant Urizen. But those who seek deeper will find more.

Blake's New Age was to be the Swedenborgian age of the 'divine human'. Early readers of Blake, unfamiliar with the Swedenborgian teachings, have supposed that because Blake has attacked certain shortcomings in his early master, he rejected the system altogether. This is not so; for 'the Divine Humanity', a phrase most readers associate with Blake, is in reality Swedenborg's, which Blake adopted together with Swedenborg's teaching that the mark of his Church of the New Jerusalem was to be the realisation of the divine in human form. If Blake is the supreme prophet of the 'God Within', he is only realising, dramatising the Swedenborgian teaching, whose unattractive bones he clothes with living form.

Only genius is able to call in question the premises of a civilization. Blake, fully aware of what was at issue, announced the mutation of an age in his challenge to the underlying assumptions of his time and ours. He knew, better than any great mind of his time (except Coleridge) what was excluded from the picture of reality drawn by the rationalists and how small the 'heaven' they were able to steal from the abyss. He knew that not their deductions, but their premises were mistaken. If as they postulated the primary reality, that by which all else is to be measured and evaluated, be matter, then the universe as described by material science follows as of course. Within their universe that vast intricate mechanism which can be described only in terms of quantity man becomes a negligible particle. This is indeed René Guénon's 'reign of quantity'.

Are there not many signs at the present time that the change of premises foreseen by Blake is already coming about? That the primacy of matter is no longer unchallenged? That, as in the Hindu and Buddhist philosophies, or in our own pre-Christian and Neoplatonic metaphysics, mind, or spirit, is again challenging that primacy? Again we find that Swedenborg lies behind Blake's passionate affirmation that eternity and infinity are not in space; his 'great eternity' is within. Life, being, bliss (the vedantic *sat-chit-ananda*) is in the smallest flower, in the little fly, the bird's heart, and within man himself, it is eternal and infinite. The essence of Blake's new premises is contained in four familiar lines,

> To see a World in a Grain of Sand
> And a Heaven in a Wild Flower,
> Hold Infinity in the palm of your hand
> And Eternity in an hour.

(K. 431)

How naive-seeming the simplicity of these lines; but how immense the intellectual wrestling with philosophic systems, with imaginative insights, which imparts to that summing up of Blake's wisdom its sublime beauty and power. Blake's infinity is not material but mental space, an immeasurable, boundless world of freedom.

If Wordsworth was the great poet of 'Nature' and the Newtonian universe, Blake is the poet who restored to man his centrality, lost with the advent of the Reign of Quantity. Wordsworth made of unpeopled mountains a national shrine; for Blake the city is the scene and the expression of the great drama of the human soul. London is 'a human, awful wonder of God.' Man becomes, once again, the creator and not the passive product of his universe; the people of London are the 'golden builders' of Jerusalem. Blake's 'London' is the London in the minds of its inhabitants; of which the outer aspect is a realisation, an embodiment; for the cities and civilizations of men are continually built and rebuilt in the likeness of our thoughts. As our industrial cities are the inhuman and dehumanising expression of the 'dark Satanic mills' of the Newtonian mechanistic philosophy, so are the Gothic cathedrals and churches Blake so loved the expressions of the spiritual vision of an age. What can be said of the featureless triviality of our contemporary conurbations?

With the advent of depth psychology and the findings of psychical research; with the study of Far Eastern religions, from the foundation of the Theosophical Society in the nineteenth century, to the adoption by the young people of the Age of Aquarius of Mantra Meditation, of the Tibetan scriptures as sacred books and the presentation of Krishna's Juggernaut in Trafalgar Square in 1973, do we not see a turning of the tide of materialist thought? Yeats, himself a leading figure in this reversal, a member of the Theosophical Society, an active experimenter in psychical research and a student of the Western esoteric tradition, translator (with his last teacher, Shri Purohit Swami) of the principal Upanishads, wrote of 'the rise of soul against intellect now beginning in the world'. Of this change Blake was both prophet and agent. He challenged Newton himself; not, of course, as a scientist or mathematician, but as a philosopher. In that respect Blake knew himself the equal of any mind. 'I *was* Socrates', he once said; 'a kind of brother'.

At least we now have the advantage over earlier readers of Blake of knowing what world we are in, as we read his Prophetic Books; twentieth century knowledge of the psyche and its structure enables us to trace our whereabouts and recognise the actors in Blake's turbulent drama in a way impossible to nineteenth century readers. It was Kerrison Preston, distinguished among the unrivalled first generation of Blake scholars, who first pointed out that Blake's Four Zoas are the four functions of the psyche as described by C. G. Jung – reason, feeling, sensation and intuition. Fourfold likewise, Blake's 'city of Golgonooza' is an example of a now familiar type of diagrammatic depiction of the structure of the psyche. Jung, who gives many examples of such diagrams drawn by his patients in the course of the process of psychic integration calls these *mandalas*; borrowing the name from those complex and beautiful Tibetan Buddhist paintings, whose purpose is to support meditation.

Some have seen Blake's mythological drama, his symbolic diagrams, as a projection of his personal conflicts and their resolution. This view was popular at a time when the theories of Freud (whose main concern was with the personal unconscious) were better known than those of Jung. But Blake's intention was to resolve not a personal but a national inner conflict. He is not the patient but the analyst.

Long before Jung Blake had written: 'All deities reside in the human breast.' To the materialist, the 'gods' are legendary heroes, or natural forces, or anything but our interior energies personified. 'Dramatisations of our moods', in Yeats's words, Jung's 'self-portraits of the instincts'. Blake had recognised, too, that these 'gods' are common to all: 'As all men are alike in outward form, So (and with the same infinite variety) all are alike in the Poetic Genius (K. 98). The gods 'reside in the human breast' and belong to a race, or a nation; and ultimately to mankind as a whole. Strange as Blake's Zoas at first appear, as they become known to us we recognise and acknowledge them, we discover them in ourselves; they are the everlasting moods or modes of the human psyche, in modern guise. The drama they enact is one in which we are immediately involved, whose resolution is in our hands.

Blake, writing in the Age of Reason, diagnosed very accurately the 'sickness of Albion,' then and now. Albion still sleeps the 'deadly sleep' of materialism imposed by those agents of Urizen, the natural reason, against whom Blake bent his 'bow of burning gold.' Bacon, Newton and Locke, together with Voltaire and Rousseau, are only earlier names by which the positivist mentality expressed itself in former centuries. The complacency of that mentality within the 'camp, court and university' (or their contemporary equivalents) is little shaken to the present day. Yet an increasing number of dissidents, with an ever-growing body of knowledge at their disposal, is calling that dominance in question.

If our argument that every culture is established in certain first principles be true, it follows that there is, for every civilization, a body of acceptable, or relevant knowledge, springing from these premises; and also an excluded knowledge. Does the relevant knowledge of one civilization become the excluded knowledge of the succeeding age? The reversal will then bring back every excluded knowledge in the fullness of time, and, in Yeats's words,

> . . . all things run
> On that unfashionable gyre again.
> *(The Gyres)*

Such areas of knowledge are excluded not perhaps deliberately, but simply disregarded as not 'knowledge' at all, within the terms of the given premises. So to the Victorians dreams were irrelevant, as were ghosts, telepathy, precognition and the like. These simply were not 'knowledge' at all, not to be explained, but only to be explained away by some Sherlock Holmes acting on his rational certainty that because these things could not be, there must be some trick which made them seem. Yet all these the twentieth century has seen come up for reconsideration in the light of a renewed attention to mind; and with renewed interest in such facts comes a re-examination of whole areas of ancient and once valued knowledge, or of the traditional and treasured wisdom of other societies. Blake was a pioneer in the re-discovery of whole areas of excluded knowledge.

For all its many inaccuracies in those details of fact so important to professional scholars, Yeats's contribution to the Ellis and Yeats commentary on Blake's symbolism is the first to have applied the right key. Yeats's commentary was itself so far in

advance of its time as to have seemed for many years an explana-
tion of the obscure by the more obscure. Himself a student of
the Western esoteric tradition Yeats recognised in Blake a fellow
initiate.

When, during the Second World War, I began my own study
of Blake I was under the impression that his 'visions' had come
to him spontaneously from 'the unconscious,' in the manner
described by Jung. This was the more credible because I was at
that time altogether ignorant of the whole body of excluded
knowledge upon which Blake drew and which Yeats had rightly
recognised in his work. Few at that time were qualified to
challenge the accepted view of Blake's 'meanness of culture' (to
use T. S. Eliot's phrase) and lack of necessary education. Because
he married beneath him and held left-wing political views and
because of the real poverty into which he sank in later years,
Blake has sometimes been presented as farther down the social
scale than in fact he was. His father was a prosperous hosier in
Golden Square (not far from Regent Street) and probably a
follower of Swedenborg, who lived much in London during his
later years. It is true that William (at his own insistence) was
not sent to school; but instead he was sent (at the age of ten)
to Pars' drawing-school, the best in London. Afterwards he was
apprenticed to Basire, engraver to the Society of Antiquaries and
other distinguished bodies. The Society's splendid series of the
Royal Tombs was in progress during Blake's apprenticeship and
Blake was the draftsman Basire sent to Westminster Abbey. These
long days working on the Royal Tombs, and in other Gothic
churches, familiarised Blake with the linear Gothic style which
he ever afterwards loved, and which so greatly influenced his own
treatment of the human figure. Works on archaeology, like Jacob
Bryant's *New System of Mythology*, with its engravings of
classical and Persian sculptures and temples, also passed through
Basire's hands; several plates in this work are thought to be by
Blake. Later, when he became his own master, Stuart and Revett's
Antiquities of Athens brought to Blake first-hand familiarity with
Greek antiquity. Thus he received the best education in, and
through the visual arts possible for any young Englishman unable
to make for the 'grand tour' of Italy himself (as did Blake's friend
Flaxman, whose origin and education were much like his own.)

As draftsman and engraver Blake thus actively participated in the most fruitful new thought of the late eighteenth century. His own affirmation that 'All Religions are One', bold as was his challenge to the current view that only the Bible is divinely inspired, was the outcome of his reading of Bryant's *Mythology* (the *Golden Bough* of its day) and other learned works of the time on Indian, Persian, Icelandic and other mythologies and religions. In the Greek revival Blake was directly involved through his professional work as an engraver. The Portland vase itself (or one of Josiah Wedgwood's replicas) was for some time in Blake's hands, while he was working on the set of engravings for Erasmus Darwin's *Botanic Garden*.

As to literacy in the ordinary sense, Blake was certainly self-educated; nor could he have had a better or more exacting master. I believe Ruthven Todd was the first Blake scholar to set himself to read every book or author Blake mentions in his writings; a mere fraction, doubtless, of the whole of his reading. Some thirty years ago I attempted the same thing myself, with transforming results. Blake had, of course, read Spencer and Shakespeare, Milton, Pope, Dryden, Gray, Young, Chapman's Homer, Percy's *Reliques of Ancient English Poetry* and his translation of Mallet's *Northern Antiquities*. He had read (in translation) the Greek and Latin poets. He had read Chatterton and *Ossian* and a host of minor eighteenth century poets – Blair, Gay, Matthew Prior and the rest, besides Geoffrey of Monmouth and other historians of the 'matter of Britain'. He had read, also, with great thoroughness those thinkers with whom he waged his life-long war – Bacon, Newton, Locke, Voltaire, Dr Johnson and others whom he saw as enemies of the imagination. In Berkeley's philosophy he found powerful arguments to use against them. The Bible he read constantly, drawing his own powerful and unorthodox conclusions:

> Both read the Bible day & night,
> But thou read'st black where I read white.
> (K. 748)

He followed his contemporaries with no less attention – Payne and Godwin, Cowper, Wordsworth and Byron. His notebook is full of penetrating comments on friend and foe alike. Dante he read first in Boyd's, later in Carey's translation, but subsequently taught himself Italian (as earlier he had learned French and some Greek) in order to read the original as he worked in the last years of his life, on the great unfinished series of illustrations to the Divine Comedy.

But all these any educated person of the time would have known. The most interesting aspect of Blake's reading lay in the depth and thoroughness with which he explored the excluded knowledge of his time, the esoteric tradition. He himself names three of his teachers – Swedenborg, Paraclesus, and Jacob Boehme. From interior evidence it is likely that he had also read Cornelius Agrippa, Thomas Vaughan (brother of the poet Henry Vaughan) and other alchemists. He had read Robert Fludd, from whom he learned something of Christian Cabbala; Thomas Burnet's *Theoria Sacra*; Stukeley's and other works on Avebury and Stonehenge; the *Hermetica* in Dr Everard's seventeenth century translation; perhaps some of the Cambridge Platonists, and several works on Gnosticism. Through the *Proceedings of the Calcutta Society* and other works by, or sponsored by, Sir William Jones, he had some knowledge of Indian myth and philosophy. One of his lost paintings was entitled 'Mr. Wilkins translating the Bhagavad Geeta' – which suggests that Blake had read the first English Translation Geeta with attention. (Flaxman designed a memorial for Sir William Jones – the design is to be seen in the Slade school – depicting Brahmans teaching Jones the Indian scriptures.) Indeed all the works of the esoteric tradition read by Blake would have furnished John M. Watkins's famous theosophical bookshop where, a century later, Yeats and others since have found their University Library of lost knowledge. Since such knowledge forms no part of the more orthodox University curricula, the academic world has long been reluctant to acknowledge that Blake (or Yeats for that matter) was learned, and deeply so, in fields of thought not accepted by the dominant culture as knowledge at all.

This has led to much misreading of Blake. His originality has been greatly exaggerated; for those very aspects of his thought which are most traditional, which are, indeed, axiomatic throughout the whole corpus of Hermetic, Gnostic, Neoplatonic and Alchemical literature, have been taken (as the case may be) for profound original insights, or mad eccentricities of the poet's own invention. His immense debt to Swedenborg has never been fully appreciated. He has been held most original where he is least so;

most eccentric where he is most derivative; most odd where he is most traditional. It might be said that for a poet to be out of step with the culture of his own society is in itself a weakness, causing a lack of grace in style and thought, or giving to Blake's writings (at worst) the character of a man talking to himself. So Blake was seen by T. S. Eliot; and this is in a measure true. But, weighed against the prodigious labour he undertook, which was to bear fruit in a coming age, we can only say that had Blake not been as he was, he would have been a less great figure.

I had not myself proceeded far in my reading of Blake's sources before I discovered that the similarity of his system to that of C. G. Jung was by no means all a matter of the unconscious. Blake's readings of Gnosticism, Alchemy, Cabbala and other branches of the excluded knowledge covered much the same ground as Jung's own. Necessarily so: for whoever seeks out that excluded knowledge will uncover the same traces, a coherent tradition from antiquity to the seventeenth century and beyond.

One may liken the lost knowledge to a submerged continent whose existence is only revealed by island summits visible above the level of 'Noah's Flood' (to use Blake's own image of the Deluge which submerged an earlier wisdom.) Little islands, scattered here and there, do not reveal the unity of the lost land of which they form a part. Blake's apparently haphazard eclecticism, bewildering and maddening as it may be to the reader who stumbles from passages on the Druids to undigested chunks of Christian Cabbala, or Boehme's or Swedenborg's *arcana* (with correspondingly abrupt changes of symbol, vocabulary and allusion) is less incoherent than it seems. Blake had a sure instinct for the several manifestations of a hidden cosmology no less coherent when fully known, than that of physical science. Jung understood, as did Yeats, the coherence and unity of this body of knowledge. So did Blake, than whom none has laboured more arduously, more ardently, to make the 'sleepers' of a materialist civilization aware of new horizons; or lost horizons resighted – those 'Atlantean Hills' whose bright summits Blake beheld rising still above the 'sea of time and space'.

Blake's eclecticism was a deliberate attempt to piece together the fragments, to demonstrate that 'all religions are one' and all myths, records of the same inner drama.

But even as a champion in the 'spiritual war' for the restoration of an excluded knowledge Blake was not unique, nor so solitary a figure as was once supposed. The most important source of his knowledge of the philosophy according to which spirit, not matter, is held to be the primary reality and foundation of the universe is the writings of the Neoplatonists and of Plato himself. These were translated into English for the first time by Blake's acquaintance and contemporary, Thomas Taylor, the Platonist.

As Taylor's works appeared, so their influence on Blake's concurrent writings is to be seen. In *A Little Girl Lost and Found* Blake retells the story of the Eleusinian Mysteries; in *The Book of Thel* his theme is the 'descent' of the soul into generation, as taught by Plotinus. Near the end of his life (1822) he made a tempera painting (now in Arlington Court, Devonshire) illustrating the Platonic theology as told by Porphyry in *De Antro Nympharum*, a mythological commentary on the Homeric Cave of the Nymphs. Blake's last work of all – a little visiting-card for George Cumberland – is an abridgement of that painting, showing the joy and freedom of the souls who plunge into the river of generated life for a season, 'To rise from generation free', enriched by experience gained on earth. Christian as he was, Blake's cosmology is, in all essential respects, Platonic. His Jesus is less the historical figure of the Church than the Platonic Logos, or (in a phrase he borrowed from Taylor) 'the true man', the Platonic Intellect or indwelling Imagination of God. Swedenborg's teaching that man's true body is his spiritual body; that the mortal body is but a 'garment', and the Resurrection is a resurrection from, not of, the flesh, is a reading of Christianity consistent enough with the Platonic theology. Blake never speaks of the 'vegetated body' otherwise than as the garment or shroud of the soul, nor did he believe in its resurrection.

These, I believe, are the aspects of Blake which have made his writings seem to many the sacred books of a new age. His blameless, courageous, and increasingly lonely life as a humble engraver, dignified and sustained at the end by the friendship of the young painters who gathered round him, is well known. He is the supreme poet of London; where (but for three tragi-comic years at Felpham under the uneasy patronage of Hayley, country squire, biographer of Cowper, poet laureate, and the most minimal of minor poets) he lived and died. His inimitable lyric gift; his powerful denunciations of the political and moral 'tyrants' of his day; the beauty of his 'illuminated books,' written, designed, engraved and illuminated by himself; these have long been well known. Rather than repeat familiar themes, or discuss Blake's place in literary history (never his concern) I have wished, in this necessarily brief and superficial Introduction, to situate Blake not in relation to standards invented by literary critics or art historians, but in terms of his own; as prophet and poet of that philosophy, 'coeval with the universe itself,' for whose restoration, at the reversal of an age, he laboured. By so doing we are better able to see Blake's place in the context of our own time; and – perhaps more significantly – this time in the context of Blake.

2 Everything that Lives is Holy

These words, repeated by Blake in more than one context, contain the essence of his prophetic message. In itself this happy phrase seems a spontaneous expression of simple delight by a mystical poet. But although in his Songs Blake can speak with simplicity to the heart of childhood he wrestled with the fundamental questions and arguments of philosophy with all the power of his great intellect, challenging the culture heroes of Western civilization and indeed the very premises upon which modern Western civilization rests. Yet he knew that he would prevail; for 'Truth can never be told so as to be understood and not be believ'd.' (K. 152)

Of course profound things are simple too, and any child can respond to the voice of life itself in the lines

> Arise, you little glancing wings & sing your infant joy!
> Arise & drink your bliss!
> For every thing that lives is holy; for the source of life
> Descends to be a weeping babe . . .
>
> (K. 289)

Blake is saying that everything that lives is holy because God is incarnate in every human life: a great and simple affirmation; words incredible, indeed quite meaningless, to those under the domination of popular atheist humanism.

Certainly it is not the view of science, in Blake's century or in our own, nor even of all professed Christians; for the churches, then as now, are only too ready to capitulate to materialist science. Deism, or as Blake more often calls it, 'natural religion', accepted the scientists' account of the 'laws of nature' which operate like a great piece of clockwork. There have been more recent models but the underlying assumption is the same – that the universe operates through natural causes and that God, except for a few questionable and arbitrary interventions called 'miracles', takes no part in its operation. This remote creator Blake contemptuously calls 'Newton's Pantocrator, weaving the Woof of Locke' (K. 483) – Newton whose account of the universe and its laws so overawed his age, and Locke the philosopher, who taught that all knowledge comes through the bodily senses. 'To mortals thy mills seem everything' Blake adds; yet he himself calls natural religion an 'impossible absurdity'. Newton was a devout Deist but Blake saw clearly that his model of a self-contained universe operating by natural law allows no place for the living God who is present 'in the lowest effects as well as in the highest causes.' Blake held the view common to all spiritual traditions that the natural world depends for its apparent existence upon causes beyond itself:

> . . . every Natural Effect has a Spiritual Cause and not
> A Natural; for a Natural Cause only seems: it is a Delusion
> (K. 513)

Not surprisingly as science gained ground the churches lost confidence; but Blake saw that the mistake of the churches lay in ever having accepted the premises of science in the first place, since by doing so they opened the way to atheist materialism. For to Blake atheism and materialism are the same thing; materialism *is* atheism, and the belief in a material universe such as the scientists describe is already atheism no matter what 'faith' in 'another world' piety may cling to. For such faith is a mistaken faith, and Blake has nothing but scorn for the belief to which the churches did, however, long to continue to cling, that

> . . . an Eternal life awaits the worms of sixty winters
> In an allegorical abode where existence hath never come.
> (K. 240)

Blake describes the god of the Deists as a self-delusion of the 'mortal worm', 'a shadow from his wearied intellect'. No longer believing in any God at all the modern materialist might still address an impersonal universe in the abject words Blake puts into the mouth of the Giant Albion (the English national being) under the domination of Bacon, Newton and Locke, and the other culture-heroes of science:

> O I am nothing when I enter into judgment with thee.
> If thou withdraw thy breath I die & vanish into Hades;
> If thou dost lay thy hand upon me, behold I am silent;
> If thou withhold thine hand, I perish like a fallen leaf.
> O I am nothing, to nothing must return again.
>
> (K. 293)

'Matter' as conceived by the materialist cannot in any sense be called 'holy'. It possesses only quantifiable properties: it can be weighed, measured, numbered, analysed and recombined. All manner of mathematical and geometrical forms and formulae can be discovered in a material universe; some scientists would go so far as to call the structure of matter 'beautiful', but to do so is to go beyond the terms of science itself and to bring in value-judgments which from a strictly scientific point of view would be called 'subjective' (which to a scientist means unreal), irrelevant to the only kind of knowledge it is possible to have of a material order. In a world of matter even human beings lose all but their quantifiable aspect and themselves become

> . . . Shapeless Rocks
> Retaining only Satan's Mathematic Holiness, Length, Bredth &
> Highth
> Calling the Human Imagination, which is Divine Vision & Fruition
> In which Man liveth eternally, madness & blasphemy against
> Its own Qualities. . .
>
> (K. 521)

So material science ever tries to impose its own identification of 'reality' with the quantifiable upon living experience, which seems to this mentality irrelevant and subjective; as Blake says 'blasphemy' against the objective standards of science. Even life and consciousness science seeks to quantify; claiming for example to have discovered something about the nature of life in observing how chromosomes are arranged in a double spiral structure. Astonishing numbers of people seem to see no distinction between the mind – a term that describes consciousness – and 'the brain,' a bodily organ that serves the mind in the same way as do other organs of the body.

If the opinion of the materialists is to be accepted, man is an animal whose existence is brief; the soul – if we are to use the word – is an epiphenomenon of matter; consciousness, a product of the brain which is a special kind of computer (a view at present very widely held); human behaviour, a matter of reflexes and habits which can be implanted or removed at the will of the government under which we live. The higher mode of being (according to the materialist philosophy) is in every case explained in terms of the lower, consciousness as a kind of electrical discharge, life as chemistry, and so on down, until with the old *fiat lux*, the mechanistic philosophy is brought to a standstill, and it begins to look as though the universe might after all prove to be a mental phenomenon, something to do with number, or a kind of waking dream. However, with the dissolution of the kind of *terra firma* which seemed to exist when scientific materialism was young, which I am old enough to remember, before 'the splitting of the atom', it is only the scientists themselves who are at yet aware of the brink on which materialism stands.

But as the scientific operation of quantifying invades ever new areas of the minute structure of matter (nature's 'labyrinths' Blake calls them) and the chemical processes of organisms we call 'living', so does the mystery of life withdraw itself. There is no point at which measurement reaches the distinct order of reality to which 'life' belongs. Science assumes continuity of degree where there is in reality difference in kind. If any Christians ever did hold an opinion so contrary to the teaching of the Gospel, (where it is said that the kingdom of Heaven is within), as that the heavens and hells are regions to be found above the clouds and in the bowels of the earth, such a notion the scientists may pride themselves on having amply disproved. One does not know whether to marvel more at the stupidity of those whose faith is shaken by astronauts' reports on outer space, or that of the materialists who fancy that they have disproved anything whatever about mental regions by exploring physical space. It is in the nature of things impossible to convert a feeling into a measurement, an idea into a chemical change in a brain-cell, consciousness to the categories of time and space, weight and measure.

Blake saw those under the domination of the materialist philosophy as like the prisoners of Plato's cave, who watch the shadows cast on the wall in front of them and take these shadows for realities. In this shadow-show honours and prizes are given among the prisoners for those who are quickest to make out the shadows as they pass and best able to remember their order, sequence, and shapes and are therefore the most successful in guessing what is to come. This describes very well the kind of materialism that observes and records the phenomena and imagines that it sees causes where it is seeing only effects.

For Blake the material body is that cave in which we are fettered and unable to turn towards the source of light and he describes with compassion the state of these caverned men:

> Ah! weak & wide astray! Ah shut in narrow doleful form,
> Creeping in reptile flesh upon the bosom of the ground!
> The Eye of Man a little narrow orb, clos'd up & dark,
> Scarcely beholding the great light, conversing with the Void;
> The Ear a little shell, in small volutions shutting out
> All melodies & comprehending only Discord and Harmony;

– discord and harmony because these can be demonstrated scientifically, whereas melody speaks to the imagination. And Blake asks:

> Can such an Eye judge of the stars? & looking thro' its tubes
> Measure the sunny rays that point their spears on Udanadan?
> Can such an Ear, fill'd with the vapours of the yawning pit,
> Judge of the pure melodious harp struck by a hand divine?
> Can such clos'd nostrils feel a joy? or tell of autumn fruits
> When grapes & figs burst their coverings to the joyful air?
>
> (K. 484–5)

But have we not all listened to the voice of the materialist philosophy persuading us that man is no more than his mortal frame:

> I am your Rational Power, O Albion, & that Human Form
> You call Divine is but a Worm seventy inches long
> That creeps forth in a night & is dried in the morning sun,
> In fortuitous concourse of memorys accumulated & lost.

It plows the Earth in its own conceit, it overwhelms the Hills
Beneath its winding labyrinths, till a stone of the brook
Stops it in midst of its pride among its hills & rivers
(K. 659)

Our great cities, of which materialist civilization is so proud, are
only worm-casts thrown up by the worms of sixty winters; our
experts responsible for these technological marvels are as vulner-
able as Goliath to the sling-stone of David the poet-king. All
their knowledge is extraneous knowledge, 'accumulated and lost',
of which we may leave records which in their turn can be fed
into new brains as into computers, to perish once more.

Plato goes on to describe what will happen when the cave-
dweller is taken out of his bonds and lifted perforce into the light
of the real world. At first the light of the sun will dazzle him, so
that he cannot give any clear account to his fellow-prisoners of
what he has seen. They will very naturally think he is mad; as
indeed Blake is sometimes even now described by those whose
norm is received opinion. If the released prisoner persists in telling
them about a world beyond their cave and makes determined
efforts to enlighten them, he will be considered subversive, and
they will probably kill him; as happened to Socrates himself.

I used to wonder, when these things were less clear to me –
and it is chiefly through Blake that they have become clearer –
just what Plato did mean when he wrote of the earth as a cave
hollowed out of the universe. Materialist theorists have their
own version to offer, of a supposedly primitive astronomy, with
the stars as holes in the revolving sphere of the heavens, and so
on. But with greater understanding we may perhaps read the
parable differently. The world is not a cave in outer space, but
space itself is a 'cave' within another order of reality. One could
more truly say that outer space is a cave in inner space. Or so
Blake understood it. While our civilization devotes its energies
to the exploration of outer space, Blake's prophetic vocation was
the re-opening of inner space – spaces of consciousness. He
wrote:

I rest not from my great task
To open the Eternal Worlds, to open the immortal Eyes
Of Man inwards into the Worlds of Thought, into Eternity
Ever expanding in the Bosom of God, the Human Imagination.
(K. 623)

Blake did not claim to possess some faculty, some extra-sensory gift that few others possess. There is all the difference in the world between those who are interested in the fringe phenomena of so-called 'supernature', and visionaries. Visionaries like Plato and Plotinus, like William Blake, call in question not the fringes and frontiers of the material world, but its foundations, the premises of materialism. Many now engaged in 'para-science' expect to discover that 'supernature' is an extension of 'nature' and look forward to the day when the kingdom of weights and measures can be extended into the world of telepathy, precognition and the rest. Just as electricity remained long undiscovered but is now perfectly familiar and no longer therefore interesting, so it will be with the 'as yet' undiscovered natural laws which will account for such things. No doubt much will be discovered on these lines.

Blake's fiery vision has nothing to do with extra-sensory perception. The vision of which he speaks is the ability to see the real nature of the things that are before our eyes, of the people we know and meet here and now in this world, of all creation, of one another and of ourselves. It is not some other world, but this world that is not as the materialists suppose; a fact which many scientists would be the first to admit since they best know how little resemblance there is between the insubstantial forces they measure and call 'matter' and the appearance of things as we see them before our eyes. They are incommensurable; there is no common measure by which the one can be compared with the other. What we see and hear and touch is an experience of consciousness. Whatever the rarified invisible energies measured by science may be is neither here nor there: the world we actually live in is not a world that can be measured or described at all in terms of quantity. It is, in Blake's words, a world of 'vision'. It is not that science has not 'as yet' explored the whole of nature, what is at issue is something more far-reaching, more fundamental. It is that science, for all its usefulness as a description of appearances is valueless as an account of the *experience* of perceiving.

Blake was the reverse of other worldly. To a clergyman who had objected to his paintings as being too 'visionary', Blake in his indignation wrote one of his wonderful letters:

I feel that a Man may be happy in This World. And I know that This World Is a World of imagination & Vision. I see Everything I paint In This World, but Every body does not see alike. To the Eyes of a Miser a Guinea is more beautiful than the Sun, & a bag worn with the use of Money has more beautiful proportions than a Vine filled with Grapes. The tree which moves some to tears of joy is in the Eyes of others only a Green thing that stands in the way. Some see Nature all Ridicule & Deformity, & by these I shall not regulate my proportions; & some Scarce see Nature at all. But to the Eyes of the Man of Imagination, Nature is Imagination itself.   (K. 793)

But is Blake really saying anything more than we all know, that what we see about us is coloured by our moods, by our subjectivity? Do we not after all see the same world whatever we may think about what we see? He means very much more than this. He is not merely giving expression to poetic enthusiasm: he means exactly what he says. For according to Blake reality is what we experience. Locke's philosophy of the five senses creates a world outside the perceiving mind; the concept of 'matter' makes a separation between mind and its object which, as Blake understood, brings into apparent existence a universe devoid of life. The mind of the 'ratio' thus creates a finite world, 'outside existence' as Blake says.

To the mortal worm, to the dweller in the Cave, 'reality' appears to be a limitless universe external to ourselves. This universe can be weighed and measured and catalogued but it remains other, it is lifeless. If other living creatures inhabit this universe we can presume that they are living and conscious beings by deduction only. Insofar as they are in that external world they are to us objects; even we ourselves are objects, like the rest. But if all that we behold exists, as Blake understood, in the human imagination – then their nature is not in space and time but in life; not finite but infinite and eternal; since space and time are conditions only of a material universe. 'He who sees the Infinite in all things, sees God. He who sees the Ratio only, sees himself only.'   (K. 98)

That the world we perceive exists in the mind that perceives it would seem self-evident to Hindu or Buddhist; as also to

Berkeley to whom Blake was much indebted, and to the Platonic tradition. It is the essence of the nature-poetry of the Old Testament, and especially of the Book of Job, that Blake knew so well, in which Behemoth and Leviathan and all the creatures of earth are presented not as products of 'nature' but as immediately and continually created by God. And Blake appeals to tradition, addressing himself to the Jews and the mystical tradition of Adam Kadmon:

> You have a tradition, that Man anciently contain'd in his mighty limbs all things in Heaven & Earth: this you received from the Druids.
> 'But now the Starry Heavens are fled from the mighty limbs of Albion'. (K. 649)

The 'starry heavens' is a clear allusion to Newton's 'telescopic astronomic heavens'; and the 'Druids' to a universal tradition of which the Jewish mystical tradition is only one branch.

But is this after all anything more than a philosopher's dispute about words? Yes it is; because existence in the human imagination, or in the Imagination of God, is living existence; different in kind from the quantitative existence of supposedly material objects in natural space. The difference is between the living and the lifeless. The world of solid matter outside mind or thought is a

> . . . rocky World of cruel destiny,
> Rocks piled on rocks reaching to the stars,
> Stretching from pole to pole. (K. 702)

When the creatures are conceived of as existing in that outer space and as part of it they seem lifeless and remote, they 'wander away' from man:

They send the Dove & Raven & in vain the Serpent over the
.mountains
And in vain the Eagle & Lion over the four-fold wilderness:
(fourfold because each of our four worlds of life has become a desert)
They return not, but build a habitation separate from Man.
The Sun forgets his course like a drunken man; he hesitates
Upon the Cheseldon hills, thinking to sleep on the Severn.
In vain: he is hurried afar into an unknown Night.

(K. 703)

The sun of daily experience, the sun that rises over the eastern hills of every man's 'garden on a mount' and sets in our own west, 'forgets his course' because abstract Newtonian astronomy has plotted for the sun a quite different course through outer space. When the sun is 'upon the Cheseldon hills' – or on whatever hills bound our 'flat earth' – he 'hesitates', because the 'globes rolling through voidness' know nothing of sunrise or sunset and their glory; there is no 'sleep' for the setting sun as it is 'hurried afar into an unknown night' of astronomic, not of human, existence. And so with the moon, and

> The Stars flee remote; the heaven is iron, the earth is sulphur,
> And all the mountains & hills shrunk up like a withering gourd.
>
> (K. 703)

– the gourd that Jonah the Prophet grieved for. They 'shrink up from existence', and have no place but in 'the void outside existence', nothing is any longer unique, no longer an identity, but only a position or a motion in abstract space. One would think that Blake had foreseen our own time, when mankind, like the rest of nature, has been quantified, when he wrote in a letter to George Cumberland (12 April 1827) that 'the majority of Englishmen are fond of the Indefinite which they Measure by Newton's Doctrine of the Fluxions of an Atom.' Whatever exists, Blake goes on to say,

> is Itself & Not Intermeasurable with or by any Thing Else. Such is Job, but since the French Revolution Englishmen are all Intermeasurable One by other, Certainly a happy state of Agreement, with which I for One do not Agree.

And Blake repeats his prayer against 'single vision' when he writes

> God keep me . . . from Supposing Up & Down to be the same thing as all Experimentalists must suppose. (K. 878)

With sorrow he contrasted the world of quantity with the world of life:

. . . A Rock, a Cloud, a Mountain,
Were now not Vocal as in Climes of happy Eternity
Where the lamb replies to the infant voice, & the lion to the man of
years
Giving them sweet instructions; where the Cloud, the River & the
Field
Talk with the husbandman & shepherd. . .

(K. 315)

In place of that dismal 'void Outside of Existence' Blake offers us a universe living with our own life, in which every thing is 'human, mighty, sublime!' (K. 665)

His demonstrations of the fallacy of materialism cover scores of pages of tough argument, of persuasive oratory, of luminous depictions of the world as it appears to the eye of the imagination.

Mental Things are alone Real; what is call'd Corporeal, Nobody Knows of its Dwelling Place: it is in Fallacy, & its Existence an Imposture. Where is the Existence Out of Mind or Thought? Where is it but in the Mind of a Fool? (K. 617)

Perhaps the title of this chapter has already explained itself. 'Everything that lives is holy' because the divine spirit in man is the ground, is the place, is the nature of all existent things when truly understood. The holiness of life is not something predicated, as an attribute, but inherent in the divine nature of the ground. The place of the world is in the ever-living Imagination and in its essence therefore both living and holy.

Consider for a moment the implications. It must surely become impossible for whoever has seen that there is nothing in creation without life or outside the life of God, to behave towards the created world as does our profane society. We kill without reason or pretext the animals and birds, poison the herbs and the insects, pollute the rivers and the seas, lay waste the earth, cut down the forests, all for material gain or expediency. If we were to see these things in terms of life, could we do these things? In the human world also – indeed above all – Blake saw the laws of 'natural religion' as 'cruel'. The laws of that world are imposed from without, whereas the law of imagination is within. Of an external

and uniform general code of conduct, such as that written on
the Mosaic 'tablets of stone' Blake wrote 'One Law for the
Lion & Ox is Oppression'. (K. 158) The new law given by
Jesus (who is the Imagination) to replace the law of Moses is the
law of imagination. 'Jesus was all virtue, and acted from impulse,
not from rules'. (K. 158) With all too good historical justification
Blake held that man's inhumanity comes about through a morality
imposed from without, whereby we treat our fellow-humans as
objects, as other, not as one in the single life of the living
Imagination. It was Blake's belief that the Imagination acts with
compassion and love where the Laws of 'natural religion' are
murderous alike of body and soul.

But a second implication has a special importance for those
concerned with the great question of immortality. Blake scorn-
fully rejected the belief of the Deists that 'Eternal life awaits the
worms of sixty winters. In an allegorical abode where Existence
has never come.' Perhaps this is the belief of some people even
now; or, more likely, that is how some people would formulate
a mystery of faith that cannot be precisely defined. But insofar
as such a belief is held in a concrete and literal sense, Blake saw
that it is untenable.

'Nature has no Supernatural & dissolves: Imagination is
Eternity.' (K. 779)

There are no heavens and hells in nature here or hereafter; they
are in mind. If we have understood, if we have even glimpsed the
import of Blake's lifelong insistence that all things exist in the
human Imagination, then we are considering a mode of being
that knows neither generation nor death, that is in its nature
immune from time and change. For mind – spirit – consciousness
– is not to be found in nature. It is not in space and therefore not
subject to the laws of nature. We not only shall be but are
already beings whose essential humanity is free from the laws
that operate only upon the physical body, which Blake calls the
'garment'. He answers the god of the natural frame,

Truly My Satan, thou art but a Dunce
And dost not know the Garment from the Man.

(K. 771)

We are not material bodies forming a part of a material mechanism but immaterial spirits in a world of life. The place where we are is not in space and time, but a place of the Imagination; an incorporeal place. We are not in space, but space in consciousness, created

> . . . in Visions
> In new Expanses, creating exemplars of Memory & of Intellect,
> Creating Space, Creating Time, according to the Wonders Divine
> Of Human Imagination. . . . .
>
> (K. 746)

Blake writes of these things not as those who put forward a hypothesis or venture an opinion; he wrote as one with knowledge. We are not mortal worms who will hereafter be promoted to immortality, but already immortal in the Imagination of God.

> Around the Throne Heaven is open'd & the Nature of Eternal Things Display'd, All springing from the Divine Humanity. All beams from him & as he himself has said, All dwells in him.   (K. 612)

Because we are already dwellers in a spiritual universe the death of the mortal body – the garment – in no way changes what we truly are.

In his account of his great composition of the Vision of the Last Judgment, he wrote:

> This world of Imagination is the world of Eternity; it is the divine bosom into which we shall all go after the death of the Vegetated body. This world of Imagination is Infinite & Eternal, whereas the world of Generation is Finite & Temporal. There Exist in that Eternal World the Permanent Realities of Everything which we see reflected in this Vegetable Glass of Nature. All Things are comprehended in their Eternal Forms in the divine body of the Saviour, the True Vine of Eternity, the Human Imagination who appear'd to Me as coming to Judgment among his Saints & throwing off the Temporal that the Eternal might be Establish'd . . .   (K. 605)

3 *Blake's Christianity*

Blake is only known to have attended a religious service three times in his life: he was baptized, in the year 1757, at the beautiful font of St. James's, Piccadilly. He was married in Battersea Old Church; and at his own wish, his burial service (he died in 1827) was according to the rites of the Church of England. His admiration for such dissenters as John Wesley and William Law notwithstanding, he preferred the national Church to non-conformity; perhaps in part because of his love for those Gothic churches – and especially Westminster Abbey – in whose architecture he saw the true expression of the spirit, in contrast with Wren's St. Paul's, which he saw as a monument to Deism and human reason. He regretted that the Reformation had divided the church.

> Remember how Calvin & Luther in fury premature
> Sow'd War and stern division between Papists & Protestants!
> (K. 507)

But he declared himself a Christian without reservation:

> I still & shall to Eternity Embrace Christianity and Adore him who is the Express image of God . . .   (K. 815)

He never had any period of doubt, early or late. But what kind of Christian was our great visionary and national prophet?

In Blake's time Anglican Christianity was dominated by Deism, or 'natural religion', which denies revelation and bases belief in God upon reasonable deduction from the phenomena of nature. What the Deists really believed in was science; their successors are our own humanists, most of whom nowadays have dispensed with deity altogether. Blake's lifelong mental fight was against Deism.

Spirit, for Blake, is not, as for the Deists, the remote first cause of a material universe but an ever-present reality creating continually all we behold. Whereas the Deists dismissed all revelation, Blake believed that all is revealed: 'To Me This World is all One continued Vision of Fancy or Imagination,' and 'Nature is Imagination itself.' (K. 793) Today when many are questioning the premises of naive materialism, Blake's spiritual religion, which he so ardently, and with such powerful argument opposed to 'natural religion' is finding followers. To his contemporaries he was incomprehensible; to a younger generation at this time he is the prophet who speaks the word of life. Blake's Jesus is the Logos, the universal eternal Mind, or Spirit, which he calls the Divine Body, or 'Jesus, the Imagination', the Imagination of God present in and to man; for 'God only Acts & Is in existing beings or Men' (K. 155)

When Blake declares his worship of 'him who is the Express Image of God' he is speaking not of the historical Jesus but rather the universal divine humanity. 'Human nature is the image of God' (K. 83) and

> Man can have no idea of any thing greater than Man as a cup cannot contain more than its capaciousness. But God is a man, not because he is so perceiv'd by man, but because he is the creator of man. (K. 90)

These quotations are taken from Blake's earliest writings. At the end of his life he was to affirm with greater assurance the same realization. In the margins of his copy of Berkeley's *Siris* he wrote:

> 'Imagination or the Human Eternal Body in Every Man . . .
> Imagination is the Divine Body in Every Man . . .'
> (K. 773)

For Blake the traditional teaching of the centrality of man in the universe is confirmed solely by the presence of God in man: 'The Eternal Body of Man is The Imagination, that is, God himself The Divine Body . . . Jesus: we are his Members' (K. 776) Thus Blake's Jesus is the archetype

. . . the Divine
Humanity who is the Only General and Universal Form
To which all Lineaments tend & seek with love & sympathy.
(K. 672)

Whereas for the humanist God is a fiction made in man's image, spiritual tradition has always taught that man is made in the image of God.

Man is the Ark of God . . . Man is either the ark of God
or a Phantom of the earth & of the water   (K. 82)

Since God is in man, his voice declares

'If thou humblest thyself, thou humblest me;
Thou also dwell'st in Eternity.
Thou art a Man, God is no more,
Thine own Humanity learn to adore,
For that is my Spirit of Life'

(K. 752)

The humanity Blake asks us to adore is not the 'phantom of earth and water' of the materialists, but the 'express image of God.' For those able to project onto an event in history their own inner experience the Christian cult has served, and may still serve to awaken our understanding. But though the historical Jesus was the teacher and exemplar of the Divine Humanity, that divinity is a reality of all being. It is for this reason, I believe, that at a time when for so many the churches seem to fail, Blake's Christianity speaks with power. Many who are at this time turning to India and the Far East would find a better guide to interior regions and experiences in the Christian teachings of 'English Blake'; not because the Eastern religions lack any of the truth Blake taught but because it is not possible to understand or live by alien symbols and practices as fully as we can understand and live by those of our own culture.

It was a teaching of Swedenborg's Church of the New Jerusalem, of which Blake and his wife (together with his friend Flaxman and his wife) were members, that the Divine Humanity is the 'God within' all humankind. 'The Heavens are in the form of a man' and the body of the Divine Humanity, since it is not in space, is neither large nor small, but universal, as the one-in-many and many-in-one of 'the Divine Family', 'One Family One

Man blessed for ever.' Swedenborg's reaffirmation of what is in reality traditional teaching – that the heavens and the hells are not in space but in mind, opening within everyone inner regions of experience, came, in the century of Locke and the Deists, as a new revelation:

> There is a Throne in every man, it is the Throne of God
> (K. 661)

Blake wrote; and it is from this Throne that Jesus the Imagination rules as the Judge and conscience of all mankind.

Doubtless Blake's seeming heresy shocked his less inspired acquaintances; like Wordsworth's friend the diarist, Crabb Robinson, who pressed Blake on his belief concerning Jesus Christ: 'He was the son of God', Blake replied; 'and so am I, and so are you.' Blake on his part denounces as idolatrous the claim of any human individual to uniqueness; even Jesus Christ and his Mother:

> . . . No Individual ought to appropriate to Himself
> . . . any of the Universal Characteristics
> . . .
> Those who dare appropriate to themselves Universal Attributes
> Are the Blasphemous Selfhoods & must be broken asunder.
> A Vegetated Christ & a Virgin Eve are the Hermaphroditic
> Blasphemy; by his Maternal Birth he is that Evil-One
> And his Maternal Humanity must be put off Eternally,
> Lest the Sexual Generation swallow up Regeneration.
> (K. 736–7)

Yet although the 'selfhoods' may not lay claim to what is universal, the universal Divine Humanity 'protects minute particulars every one in their own identity.' (K. 672). Blake's Jesus is born with every member of the human race; he is not merely human, but humanity itself, the divine image which in each of us experiences birth, the journey of life, and death.

Blake understood that it is the ego, whom he calls 'Satan, the Selfhood' – the opposite principle from Jesus, the universal Divine Humanity – who has 'wither'd up the human form' into the appearance of a multitude of little lonely separate individuals,

> Till it became a Mortal Worm,
> But O! translucent all within.

– for each of these individuals is an unique incarnation of the Divine Humanity, the indivisible All of God.

> The Divine Vision still was seen,
> Still was the Human Form Divine,
>   Weeping in weak & mortal clay,
> O Jesus, still the Form was thine.
>
> And thine the Human Face, & thine
> The Human Hands & Feet & Breath,
>   Entering thro' the Gates of Birth
> And passing thro' the Gates of Death.
>
> (K. 651)

In the matter of the human face of Jesus, Blake is shocking to some in the sheer directness with which he cuts through cant and convention. In *The Everlasting Gospel*, a late poem in which he certainly meant to provoke and shock his readers into understanding, some have thought he speaks with disrespect of Jesus Christ in the lines:

> The Vision of Christ that thou dost see
> Is my Vision's Greatest Enemy:
> Thine has a great hook nose like thine,
> Mine has a snub nose like to mine.
>
> (K. 748)

Jesus with a snub nose seems outrageous until we realize that Blake is affirming that every individual human face reflects the image of God. A more profound expression of this meaning is to be seen in the illustrations to The Book of Job. In several of these Blake has shown us simultaneously the inner and the outer worlds. Below, the story of Job, the man, is depicted; while above, we see God enthroned in Job's inner 'heavens', where the spiritual drama, with the angels and Satan, is enacted. The face of God and the face of Job are alike: for the mortal face is formed in the likeness of the God within. Every being bears outwardly the 'signature' or, to use Swedenborg's term, the 'correspondence' of its inner nature; and humanity is formed according to the archetype of the Divine Humanity.

The inner drama of redemption is reflected in human experience continually, as 'God becomes as we are, that we may be as he is,' (K. 98) following and accompanying us throughout life. Blake has his own understanding of the events of the life of Jesus, from his birth to the crucifixion. The extraordinary radiance and poignancy of all Blake's poems about infancy – Infant Joy, the Child on a cloud of *Songs of Innocence*; the Infant Sorrow who leaps into the dangerous world 'Helpless, naked, piping loud', – comes surely from his belief that in every birth the Divine Humanity is born anew. In *Jerusalem*, he describes, in a beautiful and touching image, the reflection of the single eternal event in nature's 'looking-glass' of time and space:

And Jehovah stood in the Gates of the Victim, & he appeared
A weeping Infant in the Gates of Birth in the midst of Heaven.
No Human Form but Sexual, & a little weeping Infant pale reflected
Multitudinous in the Looking Glass of Enitharmon, on all sides. . .
(K. 697)

The physical body or 'sexual garment' does not belong to the Divine Body, the Imagination, and is not the Human Form, which is spiritual. It is the 'coat of skin' in which God has clothed fallen mankind, according to the story in Genesis. Yet sex is itself made, as Blake calls it, 'holy' because through sexual love the Incarnation is perpetually realized. Blake defends sexual love as a sacrament associated with the Incarnation:

O holy Generation, Image of regeneration!
O point of mutual forgiveness between Enemies!
Birthplace of the Lamb of God incomprehensible!
The Dead despise & scorn thee & cast thee out as accursed,
Seeing the Lamb of God in thy gardens & thy palaces.
(K. 626)

When man 'shrinks' and 'withers' from his divine stature to become the mortal worm, God 'becomes a worm that he may nourish the weak' and enters Incarnation with each of us. Blake calls woman 'thou mother of my mortal part' because she clothes us in our 'sexual garments'. These we assume at what Blake calls the 'limit of contraction' – our mortal condition; and therefore he interprets the creation of the woman – Eve – as a separate being as taking place only at this 'limit'. But the curse of Eve becomes the blessing of Mary because through the 'sexual garment' woman becomes the mother of the Divine Humanity in his 'cradled infancy':

> . . . . . . the Saviour in Mercy takes
> Contractions's Limit, and of the Limit he forms Woman, That
> Himself may in process of time be born Man to redeem.
>
> (K. 670)

Blake calls Jesus the 'Saviour' and the 'Redeemer' especially when he is considering the Divine Humanity as guide and companion in the journey of life, through what he calls the States. Of these innumerable situations and states of consciousness Blake writes in an almost Buddhist sense, as signifying every condition short of supreme enlightenment: 'States that are not but ah! Seem to be '; (K. 522) and

> . . . . What seems to Be, Is, To those to whom
> It seems to Be, & is productive of the most dreadful
> Consequences to those to whom it seems to Be, even of
> Torments, Despair, Eternal Death. . . .
>
> (K. 663)

These States may be as illusory in the morally good as in the morally evil. From every state the Imagination is the "redeemer": '. . . but the Divine Mercy Steps beyond and Redeems Man in the Body of Jesus'. (K. 663) In his description of the Last Judgment Blake wrote:

> . . . it will be seen that I do not consider either the Just or the Wicked to be in a Supreme State, but to be every one of them States of Sleep which the Soul may fall into in its deadly dreams of Good & Evil when it leaves Paradise following the Serpent.　(K. 614)

Even affection and love, he warns us, becomes 'a State when divided from Imagination' but 'the Imagination is not a State: it is the Human Existence Itself.' (K. 522) Blake's States, like Dante's mountain of hells and purgatories, or like the Buddhist Wheel, are stages on a journey:

Man passes on but States remain for Ever; he passes thro'
them like a traveller who may as well suppose that the places
he has passed thro' exist no more, as a Man may suppose
that the States he has pass'd thro' Exist no more.   (K. 606)

> The Spiritual States of the Soul are all Eternal.
> Distinguish between the Man & his present State.
> (K. 681)

Hell is eternal; but no man remains eternally in hell. Jesus, the
Imagination, is said

> . . . to Create
> States, to deliver Individuals evermore!
> (K. 662)

as the ever-present possibility of release from Satan the Selfhood
into the Divine Humanity. Again and again Blake insists that

> . . . Iniquity must be imputed only
> To the State they are enter'd into, that they may be deliver'd
> (K. 680)

Satan too is a State; 'the State call'd Satan can never be redeemed
in all eternity'. The belief in the eternal damnation of any being,
even of Satan, not to mention human souls, seems to the modern
mind unbelievable; but according to Blake's understanding, 'man
passes on'; no-one remains for ever in any State, even in the
irredeemable 'State called Satan.' Insofar as each of us has an
ego, each of us has a Satan, or are in the 'State call'd Satan'.
That State is an eternal possibility; but there is no person called
Satan.

> Satan is the State of Death & not a Human Existence.
> (K. 680)

'Satan the Selfhood' is called the 'State never to be redeemed'
because it is a state of total opacity to the light of the Imagination; the 'limit of opacity', the state of death. As Jesus the
Imagination is the universal humanity, so Satan the Selfhood
includes that multitude of states of separation from the God
within which comprise the hells.

A World where Man is by Nature the enemy of Man,
Because the Evil is Created into a State, that Men
May be deliver'd time after time, evermore, Amen.
Learn therefore, O Sisters, to distinguish the Eternal Human
That walks about among the stones of fire in bliss & woe
Alternate, from those States or Worlds in which the Spirit travels.
This is the only means to Forgiveness of Enemies.

(K. 680)

Satan does not so distinguish; he is the Accuser, who imputes
sin and righteousness alike to individuals – to the ego. That is
what Blake meant when he wrote

Truly, My Satan, thou art but a Dunce,
And dost not know the Garment from the Man.
Every Harlot was a Virgin once,
Nor canst thou ever change Kate into Nan.

(K. 771)

Harlot and virgin are states; Kate and Nan are eternal individu-
alities. Satan is called the 'Accuser' because he identifies the
sinner with his sin; and therefore

. . . many doubted & despair'd & imputed Sin & Righteousness
To Individuals & not to States . . .

(K. 648)

In the poem *Milton*, Blake warns us not to identify 'the true
man' with the state he may be in:

Distinguish therefore States from Individuals in those States.
States Change, but Individual Identities never change nor cease.
You cannot go to Eternal Death in that which can never die.

(K. 521)

and he continues to urge us to subject ourselves to Judgment:

Judge then of thy Own Self: thy Eternal Lineaments explore,
What is Eternal & what Changeable, & what Annihilable.
The Imagination is not a State: it is the Human Existence itself.
Affection or Love becomes a State when divided from Imagination.
The Memory is a State always, & the Reason is a State

Created to be Annihilated & a new Ratio Created.
Whatever can be Created can be Annihilated: Forms cannot:
The Oak is cut down by the Ax, the Lamb falls by the Knife,
But their Forms Eternal Exist for-ever. Amen. Allelujah.

(K. 522)

Blake's 'Forms Eternal' are Plato's 'Ideas'.

Although there is no being called 'Satan', that state exists
wherever the empirical ego is at work, imposing its laws of
'natural religion', and he labours to expose

> . . . the Self righteousness
> In all its Hypocritic turpitude, opening to every eye
> These wonders of Satan's holiness, shewing to the Earth
> The Idol Virtues of the Natural Heart, & Satan's Seat
> Explore in all its Selfish Natural Virtue . . .

(K. 530)

In the Job engravings Blake depicts Job's most terrible ordeal as
the apparition of Satan in the guise of God, venerable and holy;
his identity revealed by his cloven foot.

But equally Blake condemned the condoning of sin by those
humanists who, like Voltaire and Rousseau teach that natural
man is good. Rousseau's *Confessions* Blake calls 'an apology &
cloke for his Sin & not a confession.' (K. 682) There have been
many since; and the permissive society is an expression of the
notion that if nothing is called sinful the problem of evil is
thereby solved. But the tolerance of vice is by no means the same
thing as the forgiveness of sin, and to condone the selfhood in
whatever it does brings us no nearer to the divine ground and
archetype.

> The Spirit of Jesus is continual forgiveness of Sin: he who
> waits to be righteous before he enters into the Saviour's
> kingdom, the Divine Body, will never enter there. I am
> perhaps the most sinful of men. I pretend not to holiness:
> yet I pretend to love, to see, to converse with daily as man
> with man, & the more to have an interest in the Friend of
> Sinners. (K. 621)

So, Blake knew, can every human being converse with the 'God Within': he claims no special privilege or right of access.

But again, the divine forgiveness operates through human beings:

> Mutual forgiveness of each Vice,
> Such are the Gates of Paradise.
> (K. 761)

Thus there are two religions: 'natural religion', which is a moral code imposed from without; and 'the religion of Jesus.' Satan's 'natural religion' is based upon the moral virtues as these are understood by the human ego, the selfhood; a cruel religion. Satan is not sinful; on the contrary, the moral code of this world is the work of the human ego, which knows no other law:

> We do not find anywhere that Satan is Accused of Sin; he is only accused of Unbelief & thereby drawing Man into Sin that he may accuse him.   (K. 615)

The ego, governed by natural reason does not believe in the kingdom of the Imagination, but only in the natural world.

> In Hell all is Self Righteousness; there is no such thing there as Forgiveness of Sin; he who does Forgive Sin is Crucified as an Abettor of Criminals, & he who performs Works of Mercy in Any shape whatever is punish'd &, if possible, destroy'd, not thro' envy or Hatred or Malice, but thro' Self Righteousness that thinks it does God service, which God is Satan . . . It is not because Angels are Holier than Men or Devils that makes them Angels, but because they do not Expect Holiness from one another, but from God only.   (K. 616)

> Satan thinks that Sin is displeasing to God; he ought to know that Nothing is displeasing to God but Unbelief & Eating of the Tree of Knowledge of Good & Evil.   (K. 615)

Blake never speaks of sin and repentance, but always of doubt, unconsciousness of the inner worlds, unbelief. Throughout history the two religions are always in the world. Satan is for ever—

Setting up Kings in wrath, in Holiness of Natural Religion

and he lists

> Arthur, Alfred, the Norman Conqueror, Richard, John,
> Edward, Henry, Elizabeth, James, Charles, William, George,
> And all the Kings & nobles of the Earth & all their Glories
>
> (K. 713)

But the spirit of prophecy creates 'around These, to preserve them from Eternal Death'

> Adam, Noah, Abraham, Moses, Samuel, David, Ezekiel,
> Pythagoras, Socrates, Euripides, Virgil, Dante, Milton
> . . .
> As the Pilgrim passes while the Country permanent remains,
> So Men pass on, but States remain permanent for ever.
>
> (K. 714)

The world-rulers and law-makers are the agents of 'natural religion', while the prophets and the poets continually express the values of the Imagination, which are not moral but human.

Blake was vigorously anti-clerical, seeing in the Churches of his day a worship of outer forms and the 'moral Christianity' of the selfhood; 'the outward ceremony is antichrist.' Self-righteousness was for him the greatest of sins. It is probably more impervious to spiritual light than vice itself, because it tends to fortify the empirical ego in its own belief in itself. It is the ego that invents moral laws; for the Imagination is its own law, as animals obey their innate instincts. But mankind, having lost access to the archetype, has no inner law to guide us, until we again return to the greater Self from which our egos have cut themselves off. This alone is sanctity, and has nothing whatever to do with morality. The living presence of God is in every man, but is not perceived by the selfhood, whose kingdom is cut off from the greater Self. Therefore the impulses which spring from the 'God Within' are condemned as morally sinful when these conflict with the moral laws invented by the ego; they obey a law of life invisible and incomprehensible to the selfhood; who adheres to the Ten Commandments written on those tablets of stone which Blake depicted in many of his paintings of the false God of the Deists. The law of the empirical selfhood is 'cruel' because from self-righteousness springs censoriousness and condemnation, persecution and war. This Blake calls 'natural religion'; it is the enemy of spiritual religion, which is the only 'religion of Jesus'. The mark of natural religion is morality; that of the spiritual religion is the continual forgiveness of sins. Neither the virtues nor the vices of the selfhood are of any significance in the light of the mystery of the divine presence.

For Blake no distinction existed between Church and State, the religious and the secular: the only distinction to be made was between the natural and the spiritual – a distinction which cuts across all institutional and conventional categories:

What is a Wife & what is a Harlot? What is a Church & What
Is a Theatre? are they Two & not One? can they Exist Separate?
Are not Religion & Politics the Same Thing? Brotherhood is Religion,
O Demonstrations of Reason Dividing Families in Cruelty & Pride!
(K. 689)

In his prophetic vision of the New Age Blake saw no place for 'stone churches', only for the Everlasting Gospel. The end of institutional religion must have seemed unthinkable in Blake's lifetime, and still remains too radical for many. Yet many spiritual seekers of today look to Blake as a teacher rather than to the churches he denounced:

. . . Go to these Friends of Righteousness,
Tell them to obey their Humanities & not pretend Holiness
. . .
Go, tell them that the Worship of God is honouring his gifts
In other men: & loving the greatest men best, each according
To his Genius: which is the Holy Ghost in Man; there is no other
God than the God who is the intellectual fountain of Humanity.
He who envies or calumniates, which is murder & cruelty,
Murders the Holy-one. Go, tell them this, & overturn their cup,
Their bread, their altar-table, their incense & their oath,
Their marriage & their baptism, their burial & consecration.
I have tried to make friends by corporeal gifts but have only
Made enemies. I have never made friends but by spiritual gifts,
By severe contentions of friendship & the burning fire of thought.
He who would see the Divinity must see him in his Children,
One first, in friendship & love, then a Divine Family, & in the midst
Jesus will appear . . .

The passage concludes with a call to Children of the New Age:

I care not whether a Man is Good or Evil; all I care
Is whether he is a Wise Man or a Fool. Go, put off Holiness
And put on Intellect. . . .

(K. 738–9)

– Intellect, of course, in the Platonic sense, as the immediate perception of truth (in contrast with the mind of the ratio which belongs to the empirical ego).

As 'Jesus, the Imagination' is 'the human existence itself' so the 'State nam'd Satan' is unreality itself, a 'kingdom of nothing' because based on illusion, since nothing exists or can exist outside God. Blake says in many passages that the State named Satan can never be redeemed; yet he also says that Jesus died to 'save Satan'. The contradiction is only apparent; for when the last soul is saved from the state of selfhood, that State will be empty and exist no more. We are reminded of the saying of the Buddha that he will not abandon this world until the last sentient being has been liberated.

The last of the States which precedes the Last Judgement Blake calls 'self-annihilation'; the putting off of the selfhood in order to enter the divine kingdom. It may seem strange that Blake saw the state of poetic inspiration as this self-negating condition, and Milton as type of the inspired poet who puts off self in vision. Not sin and repentance, but the simultaneous enlarging and annihilation of our individual selves through union with the Divine Body, is for Blake the way to Christ. This we may above all experience through poetry and the other arts; Satan is the punisher; Jesus is the sufferer of punishment;

He died as a Reprobate, he was Punish'd as a Transgressor.

(K. 494)

Satan the Selfhood makes the laws; but the Divine Human is not subject to law, being life itself. In his early and revolutionary poem *The Marriage of Heaven and Hell* Blake presents Jesus not as the maker but as the breaker of laws:

I tell you, no virtue can exist without breaking these ten commandments. Jesus was all virtue, and acted from impulse, not from rules.   (K. 158)

And at the end of his life he thought the same. In *The Everlasting Gospel* he asks a series of rhetorical questions: was Jesus gentle? Was Jesus humble? Was Jesus chaste? and so on; and he answers that

> There is not one Moral Virtue that Jesus Inculcated but Plato & Cicero did Inculcate before him; what then did Christ Inculcate? Forgiveness of Sins. This alone is the Gospel, & this is the Life & Immortality brought to light by Jesus, Even the Covenant of Jehovah, which is This: If you forgive one another your Trespasses, so shall Jehovah forgive you, That he himself may dwell among you; but if you Avenge, you Murder the Divine Image, & he cannot dwell among you; because you Murder him he arises again, & you deny that he is Arisen, & are blind to Spirit. (K. 757)

The Crucifixion also is eternally re-enacted: we ourselves crucify when we destroy in ourselves the image of God. This is the realization of Blake's Albion, who has fallen into the power of Satan the Selfhood:

> O Human Imagination, O Divine Body I have Crucified,
> I have turned my back upon thee into the Wastes of Moral Law.
>   (K. 647)

The Saviour suffers with those who suffer: but 'vengeance cannot be healed', Blake says, because

> . . . Vengeance is the destroying of Grace & Repentance in the bosom
> Of the Injurer, in which the Divine Lamb is cruelly slain.
>   (K. 648)

Finally, what, for Blake, is the meaning of the Resurrection of the Dead, through the death and resurrection of Jesus? Again, he understands the central mystery of the Christian religion as a perpetually re-enacted experience within the souls of humankind.

Believing the soul to be immortal Blake was little concerned with physical death; the corporeal body was for him only the garment of the immortal soul in its state of generation in this world.

On the design illustrating the poem *To Tirzah* (the last poem added to *Songs of Experience*) he engraved St. Paul's words, 'It is raised a spiritual body'. This text is a comment on the poem, which considers sexual generation. It opens with the lines:

> Whate'er is Born of Mortal Birth
> Must be consumed with the Earth
> To rise from Generation free.

He therefore renounces Tirzah, the 'goddess nature', as the 'mother of my mortal part.'

> The Death of Jesus set me free,
> Then what have I to do with thee?
> (K. 220)

Elsewhere he makes the Divine Humanity say

> . . . unless I died thou canst not live;
> But if I die I shall arise again & thou with me.
> (K. 743)

But the 'death' of Jesus, as Blake understands it (and in this he is rather Platonic than Christian) is his 'descent' into the 'grave' of the mortal body in order to free us from mortality. Therefore Blake addresses Tirzah as the 'mother of my mortal part' in the words Jesus used to his mother, 'Woman, what have I to do with thee?'

For Blake the only death is spiritual death. The 'sleep', 'deadly sleep', and ultimate 'death' of the soul is a death from eternity, a loss of the divine vision; and the soul's awakening from this death of spiritual oblivion is a resurrection into the Divine Body. His call is never to repent, but to awake; and this is the language rather of Plotinus than of the Church. The Platonic philosophers speak of the body as the 'cave' or 'grave' into which the soul 'descends' from eternity into the world of generation, and Blake follows them. Blake's 'funeral urns of Beulah' (Beulah is marriage) are the wombs into which souls 'descend' into generation.

There are many passages throughout his writings in which he uses the same language. Like Plato Blake believed that birth is itself a 'death' from eternity and that the assumption of a physical body brings forgetfulness. 'The Natural Body is an Obstruction to the soul or Spiritual Body' (K. 775) because the mortal body clouds the vision of the soul.

Through the very fact of birth we leave the eternal world and enter Satan's kingdom of separate selfhoods.

> Man is born a Spectre or Satan & is altogether an Evil, & requires a New Selfhood continually
> (K. 682)

and it is through the accompanying presence of the Divine Humanity who 'dies' into this world with us, that we are able to 'rise again' in Christ.

Is Blake's 'religion of Jesus' the Christianity of the Churches? In the deepest sense I believe Blake was orthodox. His was not the orthodoxy of cult or sect, but of the universality of the Everlasting Gospel, which Jesus Christ taught and of which his life was the exemplar. A cult cannot in its nature be universal; but the ground upon which Blake claims universality for his 'Jesus, the Imagination' as the Divine-Human is that Jesus is the universal Self of all mankind. To this religion all men are born; its validation is human existence itself. Since the Divine Body includes all humanity of whatever race or religion Blake can with truth write:

> Ye are united, O ye Inhabitants of Earth in One Religion, the Religion of Jesus, the Most Ancient, the Eternal & the Everlasting Gospel.   (K. 649)

> The antiquities of every Nation under Heaven, is no less sacred than that of the Jews. They are the same thing . . . How other antiquities came to be neglected and disbelieved, why those of the Jews are collected and arranged, is an

enquiry worthy both of the Antiquarian and the Divine. All
had originally one language, and one religion: this was the
religion of Jesus, the everlasting Gospel. Antiquity preaches
the Gospel of Jesus. (K. 578-9).

Blake made no distinction between Catholic and Protestant; he
admired equally St. Teresa of Avila and the French Quietists,
Fénélon and Mme Guyon with Wesley and Whitfield, naming
these

> . . . with all the gentle Souls
> Who guide the great Wine-press of Love.
> (K. 712)

He entitled an early tractate 'All Religions are One' and argued
that

> The Religions of all Nations are derived from each Nation's
> different reception of the Poetic Genius, which is every-
> where call'd the Spirit of Prophecy. (K. 98)

Even more strongly he declared himself in his marginalia to a
Deist work, Bishop Watson's *Apology for the Bible*:

> Read the Edda of Iceland, the Songs of Fingal, the accounts
> of North American Savages (as they are call'd). Likewise
> read Homer's Iliad. He was certainly a Savage in the Bishop's
> sense. He knew nothing of God in the Bishop's sense of the
> word & yet he was no fool. The Bible or Peculiar Word of
> God, Exclusive of Conscience or the Word of God Universal,
> is that Abomination, which, like the Jewish ceremonies,
> is for ever removed & henceforth every man may converse
> with God & be a King & Priest in his own house. (K. 389)

In a certain sense he believed the Jews to have received a special
enlightenment, as he declares in the *Marriage of Heaven and Hell*,
putting the words into the mouth of the Prophet Ezekiel

> . . . we of Israel taught that the Poetic Genius (as you now call
> it) was the first principle, and all the others merely derivative,

which was the cause of our despising the Priests & Philosophers of other countries, and prophecying that all Gods
would at last be proved to originate in our & to be the
tributaries of the Poetic Genius . . . This . . . is come to
pass; for all nations believe the Jews' code and worship the
Jews' god, and what greater subjection can be?
(K. 153–4)

Jesus, as the Imagination itself, is the embodiment and fullest
expression of the Jewish prophetic tradition. At the same time
his mission was to remove what Blake calls 'the Jewish imposture'
which claims uniqueness in what is universal. The same criticism
might be made of the Christian Churches.

4 *Blake's Last Judgment*

Every civilization except perhaps our own has borne witness in its art to its knowledge and experience of a universal and unanimous tradition of spiritual wisdom. The art of the present time testifies not to knowledge of, but ignorance of this wisdom, by which all great ages have lived and died, and which a new generation is now it seems beginning to rediscover; with singularly little help from Church or University, but much from William Blake.

And yet spiritual knowledge is no less objective, no less verifiable than is the scientific knowledge upon which our culture is founded; and in which even the Church, now bent on 'demythologizing' itself, appears to have more real faith than in the Christian doctrine it daily proclaims, that Christ 'shall come again in glory to judge both the living and the dead.'

Before symbols disappear altogether their meaning is forgotten or falsified; and so it is with the awful splendour which once invested the Church's teaching of a Last Judgment. Not an exclusively Christian conception, it is also Platonic, Egyptian, Buddhist, Hindu; in spite of which humanists take excessive credit for their perspicacity in disbelieving what no Christian who understood his own religion would ever believe: that at the end of the world, all the churchyard turf will heave, as in Stanley Spencer's painting of the General Resurrection at Cookham, as the bodily dead rise up for a grand trial before a high court judge, from whose verdict there is no appeal. Kafka took for his theme *The Trial*, which ends with the death-sentence carried out upon the hero K, who from first to last has protested his innocence, not knowing in the least for what he is being tried, nor by whom, nor why.

But for Blake the Judgment was quite otherwise understood.

The Last Judgment is not Fable or Allegory, but Vision
. . . . Vision or Imagination is a Representation of what
Eternally Exists, Really and Unchangeably . . . The Last
Judgment is one of these Stupendous Visions. I have repre-
sented it as I saw it; to different People it appears dif-
ferently as everything else does . . .   (K. 604–5)

He doubted neither the certainty of the event, nor its justice,
nor its mercy. For him it lacked nothing of its traditional terror,
nor its traditional glory; yet at the same time he saw the Last
Judgment as a joyous and liberating disillusionment, like waking
from a bad dream.

The Last Judgment is an event which takes place in the inner
kingdom; for the heavens and hells are all within ourselves, as
the Gospel teaches: 'the Kingdom of Heaven is within you.' For
Blake the Judgment is a crisis of consciousness; the ultimate
crisis of consciousness.

The idea that our conscious self is by no means our whole
self is nowadays familiar, and in whatever the various schools of
psychology may differ all are agreed that we are normally aware
of only a small part of what is in us. Consciousness is like a small
circle of light beyond which lie regions of memory, some recover-
able at will, some not; and beyond our personal memories, archetypal configurations and unknown energies of the psyche. Beyond
everything which we can still, however remotely, call ourselves,
there is what the mystics have called the 'divine ground'; the
presence in, and to, the human soul, of what can only be named
God.

The true centre of the psyche, called by Jung (who takes the
term from Indian philosophy) the 'Self', or 'Transpersonal Self'
is not the ego. In Blake's language, it is the 'Divine Humanity',
the Imagination, the 'God Within'. And however we may differ
in our outward personalities, the indwelling Imagination is the
same in all and so are certain innate archetypes or 'Divine
Images', as Blake calls them. Jung named this shared archetypal
inheritance the 'collective unconscious', a clumsy term which
does small justice to Blake's 'images of wonder' which inhabit
those inner worlds.

If the Spectator could Enter into these Images in his
Imagination, approaching them on the Fiery Chariot of his

Contemplative Thought, if he could Enter into Noah's
Rainbow or into his bosom, or could make a Friend &
Companion of one of these Images of wonder, which always
intreats him to leave mortal things (as he must know), then
would he arise from his Grave, then would he meet the Lord
in the Air & then he would be happy.   (K. 611)

('Noah's Rainbow' because the 'flood of the five senses'
drowned mankind's perceptions of the spiritual world, and the
rainbow is the sign of promise, the shimmering beauty of the
spectrum which links a lost spiritual vision to the earthly, in our
post-diluvian world.)

What Jung calls the Transpersonal Self Blake calls 'the true
vine of eternity'; for Jesus Himself says, 'I am the vine and ye
are the branches', the one life in all.

Among Blake's archetypal images of the inner world the vision
of the Last Judgment occupies a special place; for it is a total
vision, or epiphany, of the archetypal order, as a whole. In this
sense it is the term of human consciousness, not a station on the
way; nor is it merely an event which takes place at the end of the
world: it is itself that end; for it is the total and ultimate confrontation of the temporal with the eternal, the part with the
whole.

Why we have not at all times access to the 'other' mind is a
mystery which the several religious traditions have variously
attempted to explain. From that indwelling spirit we are cut off,
according to the Buddhists, by ignorance; who teach not repentance but enlightenment. Plato taught in parable that the souls
about to enter incarnation must each drink from the waters of
Lethe, the River of Forgetfulness. According to Neoplatonic
commentators this river is matter. As we drink more or less deeply
so do we more or less completely forget what we knew in eternity.
The Platonic admonition is to remember; and Blake agrees. His
call is never to repentance from sin, but always to awake from our
'deadly sleep' which is little short of spiritual death itself. The
Last Judgment is not a moral trial but an awakening.

That we are in the predicament of limited consciousness is more
evident than how we fell into it. Although Blake rejects the
moralistic terms of Deism he does nevertheless lay on us the
responsibility for our condition. Kafka's K. – in this a true

successor of the Hebrew tradition of Job who pleaded his innocence before Jehovah – could never be brought to admit, in his Trial, that he was in any way blameworthy; yet it is not only in the Judaeo–Christian tradition that we are held to be responsible. The Indian religions teach the law of Karma – we reap what we sow, and as we make ourselves in one life so are we born in another. Plato fables that the souls are warned before they leave eternity not to drink too deeply of the River of Forgetfulness. Blake also lays the responsibility on us because we have chosen the mind of the ratio – of the empirical selfhood – thus losing the imaginative vision:

> If the doors of perception were cleansed every thing would appear to man as it is, infinite.
> For man has closed himself up, till he sees all things thro' narrow chinks of his cavern.   (K. 154)

'Sense is the Eye of Imagination', he elsewhere says; but when natural reason persuades us to see 'with not through the eye' (K. 433), the senses no longer serve the imagination but the natural empirical ego. It is by the mere removal of 'error' that a world created by a fallacy is, according to the tradition that the world ends in fire, 'burned up':

> Error, or Creation, will be Burned up, & then, & not till then, Truth or Eternity will appear. It is Burnt up the Moment Men cease to behold it.   (K. 617)

'Error, or Creation' is merely a misconception of 'Truth or Eternity'. Blake understood that the eternal is not something beyond and outside this existence but the real nature of things:

> Many suppose that before the Creation All was Solitude & Chaos. This is the most pernicious Idea that can enter the Mind, as it . . . Limits All Existence to Creation & to Chaos, to the Time & Space fixed by the Corporeal Vegetative Eye, & leaves the Man who entertains such an Idea the habitation of Unbelieving demons. Eternity Exists, and All things in Eternity, Independent of Creation which was an act of Mercy.   (K. 614)

'Time is the mercy of eternity' he elsewhere says; a living space in which our fallen humanity can work out its own salvation.

Explain it as we may, this sense of having lost, or forgotten, some knowledge we once possessed, or almost possess; of some greater consciousness which haunts us and seems to hover on the fringes of our awareness, is an experience we all know. Evolutionists would say that we have never possessed this greater awareness, but that it presses in on us as a coming-to-be. The perennial philosophy according to the Platonists, the Christian theologians and Blake, sees this sense of loss as being in fact the loss, the lapse which we feel it to be. Wordsworth, paraphrasing Plotinus, wrote that

> Our Birth is as a sleep and a forgetting:
> The soul that rises with us, our life's star,
> Hath had elsewhere its setting
> And cometh from afar;
> Not in entire forgetfulness.

However modern psychology might explain a universal intuition that our present consciousness is incomplete and defective, both Freudian and Jungian schools have adopted the Platonic term, *anamnesis* – recollection, more literally un-forgetting – which describes the process in which they too see the way to self-discovery. Knowledge, Plato says, comes to us by bringing to mind what is already there; and the psychologists say much the same; what is already present in our own or in the collective 'unconscious', comes to us like a memory of what we already and for ever know. The Platonic philosophers indeed reverse the terms of our modern psychology; for them it is we who are 'unconscious', while the eternal mind is omniscient.

Blake believed the same:

> In my Brain are studies & Chambers fill'd with books & pictures of old, which I wrote & painted in ages of Eternity before my mortal life; & those works are the delight & Study of Archangels. (K. 802)

Blake followed the Platonists and anticipated Jung in his belief that archetypal forms are innate; and the reawakening of our lost world of consciousness, submerged by 'the flood of the five senses', was the end for which he laboured.

> The Nature of my Work is Visionary or Imaginative; it is
> an Endeavour to Restore what the Ancients call'd the
> Golden Age.   (K. 605)

In terms of Blake's mythological language, the Golden Age of
the Greeks, the Lost Paradise of the Hebrew myth, is a lost mode
of consciousness. The restoration of this lost consciousness is the
Last Judgment; which is nothing less than the confrontation of
the temporal world of 'Error, or Creation' in which each of us has
imprisoned himself, in which we are shut in like the dead in their
graves, with 'Truth or Eternity.'

Most of the prose passages quoted above are taken from
Blake's notebook for the year 1810, from his description of his
painting of the Last Judgment. Several pencil-sketches also exist,
besides a shorter description, written in 1808. To this theme
Blake returned again and again. The ninth Night of *Vala* or *The
Four Zoas* (1795–1804) describes, in Blake's polytheistic
Christian mythology, a Last Judgment; Jerusalem, his last prophetic poem (1804–20) concludes with a Last Judgment; and
the theme is also treated (from another point of view) in *The
Everlasting Gospel*. *Milton* deals with one significant aspect of
this event, the part played in it by poetic inspiration. The twenty-
two illustrations to the Book of Job describe the judgment of the
individual man; whereas in his final pictorial version of this great
theme, on which he was still working in the year of his death
(1827) he depicts the judgment of the whole human race.

Blake greatly admired Michelangelo's Judgment and his own
composition shows many borrowings; the headlong falling figures
of a group of the damned (Blake had already used the same
image in his Job) come from Michelangelo. And yet this painting
bears more resemblance to a Tibetan mandala than to anything
in Western art. All mankind is shown as if cells flowing and
circulating within the one life of the cosmic Christ, the one in
many and many in one.

Blake has written a detailed description of the symbolism of
every figure or group of figures in this composition. The detail
need not concern us. It is necessary only to say that he has taken
all or nearly all these figures from the Bible, not as unique
persons but as types of all the possible human situations or 'states'
which recur in generation after generation.

It ought to be understood that the Persons, Moses & Abraham, are not here meant, but the States signified by those names, the Individuals being representatives or Visions of those States . . .   (K. 607)

Blake also wrote an account of Chaucer's Canterbury Pilgrims, in which he repeats the same idea –

The characters in Chaucer's Pilgrims are the characters which compose all ages and nations: as one age falls, another rises, different to mortal sight, but to immortals only the same; for we see the same characters repeated again and again, in animals, vegetables, minerals, and in men; nothing new occurs in identical existence; Accident ever varies, Substance can never suffer change nor decay.   (K. 567)

Therefore in this great multitude of figures Blake has sought to depict the whole range of human passions and states of being, the joyous and the sorrowful and the glorious, the enlightened and the dark; all within the single life of the Divine Humanity in which all live.

The 'eternal Realities as they Exist in the Human Imagination' are all experiences of humanity, all the 'States' exist in the unity of the Divine Humanity; and there is no state but some man or woman has lived it; 'there is not an Error but it has a Man for its Agent, that is, it is a Man' (K. 615): and around the Throne we see innumerable human beings each making real some state of good or evil, or error or of truth. These states are the potentialities of the human imagination in and by whom they are created.

Jesus is surrounded by Beams of Glory in which are seen all around him Infants emanating from him; these represent eternal Births of Intellect from the divine Humanity.

(K. 613)

In truth every infant born is the realization of some possible idea that potentially exists with the Human Imagination. The 'innumerable multitudes of eternity' for ever extend and realise the kingdom of the Divine Human. The one life is in us all; and it is we who are the travellers, we who like Dante travel through all the hells and the heavens and the purgatories of the human condition. 'Man passes on' but states eternally remain as possibilities. Only in this sense, according to Blake, are the hells eternal.

The Last Judgment is the supreme enlightenment, before which all the relativities of Good and Evil fade like a dream; as was the case with Job who, when God showed himself in the whirlwind found that all his questions concerning good and evil were not so much answered as totally removed.

To Blake, the Last Judgment is enlightenment, it is the opening of our inward sight which enables us to see things as they really are. That is why it is the 'last'; for it is absolute, no further possibility remains for opinion or speculation. Job and his friends argued about God and justice through thirty chapters; but when God appeared in the whirlwind there was no more argument. 'I have uttered that I understood not', Job answers God; 'but now mine eyes seeth thee.' What has happened to Job is that illumination variously described in all the great world-religions; the cosmic vision of Arjuna in the Bhagavad Geeta; or the Buddhist state of enlightenment; the beatific vision of the Christian saints.

Traditionally the Judgment is believed to be undergone by every soul after death; this belief was held in ancient Egypt, and Plato's writings on the after-life contain the same teaching. The *Dies Irae* – that great hymn in which the terrors of the Judgment are announced – was sung at the Mass for the dead; for at death each soul is held to stand before the Judge, stripped of all temporal refuge or concealment. This Blake too doubtless believed; for him the immortality of the soul was a truth beyond question. But the Judgment is also continuous, though veiled; every moment of time stands before the eternal. The Last Judgment is an ever-present reality, hidden only by the degree of our own unconsciousness, or mortal 'sleep', 'deadly sleep' or 'death', as Blake says, using the Neoplatonic language to describe the mortal condition. To whoever perceives the eternal order, the temporal stands already judged in the light of eternity.

Blake keeps faithfully to the traditional and familiar Christian symbolism; when 'Jesus the Imagination' appears upon his Throne, the temporal world is consumed in fire, as the dead rise from their graves before the Judge, who is the Imagination present in and to every human consciousness. Blake's Judgment is not a judgment of the moral law, as this is understood in the temporal world ('Satan's Kingdom'): it is none the less terrible since it is a judgment of all false constructions by reality itself; of every soul by 'the God Within'. Against such a Judgment there can be no appeal, for we judge ourselves.

The 'dead' who rise from their 'graves' are the souls who have 'descended' (in Platonic terms) into the cave, or 'grave' of mortal life; they are the living-dead who, as in *Ah! Sun-flower*

> Arise from their graves, and aspire
> Where my Sun-flower wishes to go.
> (K. 215)

From the 'graves' of our mortality our true selves, however long buried under habit and cares, must finally 'arise'.

The Last Judgment begins when the 'cloud' – of ignorance, of sleep, of unconsciousness – opens and rolls away to reveal the presence of the Divine Human, 'the Human Imagination' who is the true humanity in all men. When in the Christian creed it is said that 'He shall come again in glory to judge both the living and the dead' it is not from without but from within that He shall come. This is the vision that Blake has depicted;

> The Cloud that opens, rolling apart before the Throne & before the New Heaven & the New Earth.   (K. 612)

We shall then for the first time see that the new heaven and new earth have been there always; it is we who, being renewed, see with new eyes.

> The Graves beneath are open'd, & the dead awake & obey the call of the Trumpet; those on the Right hand awake in joy, those on the Left in Horror.   (K. 609)

The resurrection is within ourselves. To Blake this was the awakening supremely to be desired; but not all truly desire to see God. On the contrary, it is the last thing that the usurping ego, 'Satan the Selfhood', wants; for that vision brings down all our false constructions, our self-deceptions, our self-righteousness and our false personalities, in ruin. For some, as for Blake, the summons of that Trumpet brings joy; but there are others who are so deeply committed to disbelief, to some ideology, or self-centred emotional attitude, that the aspect of things as they are, seen in this illumination, must come as a shock so profound that we can only see with horror that whole false edifice of Satan the Selfhood crumbling into dust or going up in flames. Not everyone is glad; perhaps no-one is so wholly selfless as to be wholly glad. Perhaps we are all at once the saved and the damned – the Satan in each of us consigned to the flames, while the Imagination in each of us, the Divine Human, is freed.

This transformation of consciousness is not reached by discovery, speculation or experiment, but by an opening from within, by 'revelation' Jesus appears,

> . . . the Heavens opening around him by unfolding the clouds around his throne.   (K. 606)

Earth and Heaven (Blake follows Swedenborg's definition of these as the outer and the inner objects of consciousness) are renewed by a renewal of consciousness itself; not by progress or evolution, still less by learning or by experiment, but by revelation – epiphany – the objects of imaginative knowledge appear before consciousness. The 'cloud' is our own clouded awareness. When Yeats wrote in his introduction to the first version of *A Vision* that 'truth cannot be discovered but it may be revealed' he was speaking of imaginative 'truth or eternity' in Blake's sense.

Many persons have refused to accept the Christian teaching of an eternal hell for the wicked and an eternal heaven for the righteous because the 'cruelty' implicit in such a judgment is incompatible with the idea of a God who is both merciful and supreme in power. Blake too held moral judgment to be cruel.

Blake believed, in accordance with the traditional teaching of the Christian Church, that the heavens and hells are eternal; but not that anyone need remain in them eternally; only that the possibilities are always there, in every age, for every human being, because they are possibilities of experience inherent in our nature.

Night the Ninth of *The Four Zoas*, 'Being the Last Judgment', is Blake's first version of his great theme. The elaboration of mythological detail is constructed upon a very simple and orthodox foundation. The trumpet sounds, and at the cry of the time-spirit, Los, 'Awake, ye dead, & come To Judgment', the earth is shaken, the dead rise trembling from their graves, tyrants fall, while the blessed rejoice:

> Folding like scrolls of the Enormous volume of Heaven & Earth,
> With thunderous noise & dreadful shakings, rocking to & fro,
> The heavens are shaken & the Earth removed from its place,
> The foundations of the Eternal hills discover'd.

(K. 357)

But it is Satan 'the prince of this world', 'the soul of the natural frame', the individual and the collective ego, who metes out moral judgment and punishment in the endless persecutions, wars and bloodshed of the temporal world. Paradoxically, the Last Judgment is the discarding of the very notion of moral judgment. The illusion which Blake's Job had to discard was that God is a moral God, rewarding the just and punishing the wicked. That moral tyrant, Blake roundly declared, is Satan the Selfhood, the human ego. It is we who make the moral laws and a corresponding system of rewards and punishments. But God is the supreme living reality whose ways transcend human understanding; and who nevertheless abides in men, who is life of every life. When we stand before the God within, we are judged, condemned and forgiven in one supreme moment of truth.

The experience is a transformation of consciousness; the illusory 'Creation' which is brought into being through an imprisoning and narrowing of consciousness, a closing of the doors of perception till man 'sees all things thro' narrow chinks of his cavern', now is 'burned up': Heaven and earth now appear not as solid matter but as 'scrolls', a record written and read by the mind. The 'place' of the earth is no longer, as formerly supposed, physical space; from that place earth is 'removed', and 'the foundation of the Eternal hills' is 'discovered' to be in mind itself; for 'This World, is all One continued Vision of Fancy or Imagination'. (K. 793) Whatever belongs to the false constructions of the illusion of the ratio is 'consumed' in the 'fire' of vision; while whatever belongs to eternity is released as from a prison, by the supreme experience which humanity at once desires and fears:

> From the clotted gore & from the hollow den
> Start forth the trembling millions into flames of mental fire,
> Bathing their limbs in the bright visions of Eternity.
>
> (K. 359)

'Clotted gore' is the mortal body and the 'hollow den' the Platonic cave.

The reaping of the harvest of earth into the barns of Eternity employs the Eleusinian emblem of immortality – the ear of corn – which St. Paul used when he preached to the Greeks the Christian doctrine of the Resurrection. 'Unless a grain of corn fall onto the ground and die' any initiate of the Mysteries would have understood: mortal life is a 'death' from eternity; 'and who knows whether to live be not to die, and to die to live' was said also by Plato. Blake is alluding to both Christian and Platonic traditions in his fine image.

> And all Nations were threshed out, & the stars threshed from their
> husks.
>
> (K. 374)

– for the 'stars' are a Platonic symbol for the souls who 'descend' or who are (according also to the Christian parable) 'sown' on earth; and the 'husks' the natural body from which the spiritual body is raised.

The wine-press too is both Dionysian and Christian; and as the 'stars' are threshed from their 'husks' so the 'clusters of human families' fall 'howling' into the wine-press while the distilled 'odours' (the Dionysian symbol of the reascent of the soul) sing as they rise:

> O terrible wine presses of Luvah! O caverns of the Grave!
> How lovely the delights of those risen again from death!
> O trembling joy! Excess of joy is like Excess of grief.
>
> (K. 376)

There is a passage in *The Everlasting Gospel* so shocking to conventional Christian sensibilities that one Christian commentator (Mrs. Margaret Bottrall) has gone so far as to suggest that the words to Jesus which appear to be spoken by God are spoken by 'The God of this world', Satan:

> If thou humblest thyself, thou humblest me;
> Thou also dwell'st in Eternity.
> Thou art a Man, God is no more,
> Thy own humanity learn to adore,
> For that is my Spirit of Life.
> Awake, arise to Spiritual Strife
> And thy Revenge abroad display
> In terrors at the Last Judgment day.
> God's Mercy & long Suffering
> Is but the Sinner to Judgment to bring.
> Thou on the Cross for them shalt pray
> And take Revenge at the Last Day.
> This Corporeal life's a fiction
> And is made up of Contradiction.
>
> (K. 752–3)

A difficult passage, certainly; but one which contains so many elements of Blake's thought that we must accept it as it stands. We may begin with the reply of Jesus:

> I never will Pray for the World.
> Once I did so when I pray'd in the Garden;
> I wish'd to take with me a Bodily Pardon.

Blake is here using the words of St. John's Gospel (17.9) to establish his argument that 'Jesus the Imagination' does not save the world, but saves *from* the world:

> I pray for them: I pray not for the world, but for them which thou hast given me; for they are thine. And all mine are thine, and thine are mine.

Jesus does not save 'error or Creation' because 'This Corporeal life's a fiction'; it has no reality in it, and therefore vanishes, as an illusion vanishes, in the light of reality. A 'bodily pardon' is an impossibility. The Last Judgment is described in *Jerusalem* as an awakening from a dream:

> O pitious Sleep, O pitious Dream! . . .
>
> (K. 742)

The word which it seems hard to associate with the divine mercy is 'revenge', twice repeated. It must however be read in the context of a poem whose purpose is to portray a Jesus neither humble nor meek, and to destroy the insipid image of the Jesus of popular imagination. If the foregoing account of the Last Judgment is borne in mind, its terrors, for Satan's Kingdom, which is the temporal world, are real enough: and might be called the 'revenge' of spiritual reality upon the oppressors of spirit who in this temporal world wield power. Christ, in Cabalistic terms, is, as the Judge, Geburah (justice) rather than Chesed (mercy). The revenge, however, is not everlasting torment, but the destruction of a texture of illusion to which the temporal man wrongly clings.

As to the lines

> God's Mercy & Long Suffering
> Is but the Sinner to Judgment to bring

– these words do in fact describe what Blake conceived to be the whole purpose of the 'six thousand years' of the temporal experience: for the Judgment is the supreme, the ultimate experience of awakening. 'Time is the mercy of Eternity.' (K. 510) 'Canaan' (the six-thousand years) is 'mercifully' created 'to protect Satan from punishment' while fallen mankind can work out his salvation. It is Satan, the Selfhood, who alone must, at the Last Judgment, be destroyed or redeemed (which is the same thing); for in either case, he disappears from the picture. This creation of a time-world is repeatedly called 'an act of Mercy'. To this theme, as an essential part of the scheme of salvation, Blake often returns; it forms an important part of the mythological structure of *Milton*. This time-world is a dream; its duration is less than a moment of Eternity:

> Every Time less than a pulsation of the artery
> Is equal in its period & value to Six Thousand Years.
> (K. 516)

Eternity is ever-present; and to its confrontation and Judgment all, soon or late, must come.

In reading Blake's account of the Last Judgment it seems

strange to find him as it seems disgressing into a discussion of art:

> No man can Embrace True Art till he has Explor'd & cast out False Art (such is the Nature of Mortal Things), or he will be himself Cast out by those who have Already Embraced True Art . . . Whenever any Individual Rejects Error & Embraces Truth, a Last Judgment passes upon that Individual.   (K. 613)

The logic of the transition from art to the Last Judgment is not at first sight apparent. It is a measure of the disrepute into which the arts have (on the whole deservedly) fallen at this time that their mention seems out of place in the context of humanity's ultimate spiritual enlightenment. But to Blake the arts are representations of imaginative reality, the means by which we are able to make visible and audible the immaterial, invisible inner world of the human spirit.

> Poetry, Painting & Music, the three Powers in Man of conversing with Paradise, which the Flood did not sweep away . . .   (K. 609)

Water, worldwide symbol of matter and its unstable flux, 'the sea of time and space', gave Blake the meaning he attaches to Noah's Flood, which drowned the inhabitants of the earth in the philosophy of the five senses. He depicted Newton, type of materialist science, working on diagrams spread out on the floor of the sea of matter in which he is submerged. Through the arts we may still discover the hidden Self beyond the empirical selfhood. 'Paradise' is not a place to be discovered by the exploration of this or any other world situated in space and time; only by enlarging our capacity for experience – by exploring our own living inner worlds – can we enlarge our universe in any significant way; and because the arts have the power to lead us to this state, Blake would have every man an artist.

> A Poet, a Painter, a Musician, an Architect: the Man Or Woman who is not one of these is not a Christian. You must leave Fathers & Mothers & Houses & Lands if they stand in the way of Art.

> Prayer is the Study of Art.
> Praise is the Practise of Art.
> Fasting etc., all relate to Art.
> The outward Ceremony is Antichrist.
> The Eternal Body of Man is the Imagination, that is
> God himself ⎞
> The Divine Body ⎠ ישׁ[ו]ע, Jesus: we are his Members.
> It manifests itself in his Works of Art (In
>   Eternity All is Vision)
>
> (K. 776)

There are two kingdoms: the kingdom of this world whose Lord is Satan the Selfhood, 'the mind of the natural frame'; and the kingdom of Imagination. Nature is measurable, divisible, quantifiable; the kingdom of Imagination is indivisible, immeasurable, invisible, free of time; its Lord is 'the living God'. It is the human kingdom for it exists within human consciousness. The knowledge proper to the mind of the natural frame is quantitative and scientific, it is discovered by experiment and stored in memory. The knowledge proper to Imagination is knowledge of that truth 'vision', which (in Yeats's words) 'cannot be discovered but may be revealed'. Its expression is to be found in the arts and religions of all nations. Thus the arts are vital to that aspect of our existence which is specifically human, unshared by mineral, vegetable or animal. They are the sole means by which we may communicate knowledge of the spiritual world, the specifically human kingdom.

As there are two religions – 'natural religion' whose concern is the application of moral law in the natural world; and 'the religion of Jesus' – who is the Imagination – so there are two kinds of art. For it is inevitable that in a world dominated by materialism there should be a materialist art as there is a materialist religion, Deism. The Greek fable of the contest of the Muses and the Magpies was no doubt in Blake's mind when he wrote of the 'daughters of memory' and the 'daughters of Inspiration.' (The outcome of the contest was the triumph of the Muses and the disgrace of the Pierides; at present the prizes would doubtless go to the magpies as being less 'obscure' and appealing to 'a wider audience.')

The Last Judgment is not Fable or Allegory, but Vision. Fable or Allegory are a totally distinct & inferior kind of

Poetry. Vision or Imagination is a Representation of what Eternally Exists, Really & Unchangeably. Fable or Allegory is Form'd by the daughters of Memory. Imagination is surrounded by the daughters of Inspiration . . . The Hebrew Bible & the Gospel of Jesus are not Allegory, but Eternal Vision or Imagination of All that Exists. Note here that Fable or Allegory is seldom without some vision. Pilgrim's Progress is full of it, the Greek Poets the same; but Allegory & Vision ought to be known as Two Distinct Things, & so call'd for the Sake of Eternal Life. (K. 604–5)

For the sake of eternal life because if the distinction is forgotten and confused the essential nature and use of visionary art is forgotten and the human kingdom of the Imagination is lost. This comes about whenever the attempt is made to reduce differences of kind to difference of degree:

Some People flatter themselves that there will be No Last Judgment & that Bad Art will be adopted & mixed with Good Art, That Error or Experiment will make a Part of Truth, & they boast that it is its Foundation; these People flatter themselves: I will not flatter them. Error is Created. Truth is Eternal. (K. 617)

The Daughters of Memory belong to the world of the ratio, not to the world of life. Their work Blake calls 'false art' because, however clever or elegant it may be, it performs no essential function; whereas through 'inspiration' alone is Imagination – the 'other' mind – able to communicate with our limited human consciousness. The arts therefore have, according to Blake, a necessary part to play in bringing to us the vision of eternity.

To this existential confrontation we are forced, so he believed, by the exhaustion of all temporal possibilities:

When Imagination, Art & Science & all Intellectual Gifts, all the Gifts of the Holy Ghost, are look'd upon as of no use & only Contention remains to Man, then the Last Judgment begins. (K. 604)

When the Last Judgment begins differences formerly thought to be merely of degree are seen to be differences in kind. Therefore it is by no means a digression when Blake concludes his account

, Jesus: we are his members.

of the Last Judgment with a call to reject 'Bad Art', the work of the daughters of Memory, and to embrace 'Good Art'. Blake has a way of becoming disconcertingly matter-of-fact when we expect him to soar beyond our sight. He does not spare us by allowing us to suppose that what he is discussing is beyond our ken. A Last Judgment, he says, is necessary only because 'fools flourish'. If we had kept the vision of our childhood – the state he calls 'Innocence' – no shattering revelation, no sweeping away of our false opinions and constructions would have been necessary at all.

> Men are admitted into Heaven not because they have curbed & govern'd their Passions, or have No Passions, but because they have Cultivated their Understandings. The Treasures of Heaven are not Negations of Passion but Realities of Intellect, from which all the Passions Emanate Uncurbed in their Eternal Glory.   (K. 615)

Natural religion is moral; but the religion of the Imagination has nothing to do with morality; the measure of imaginative truth is something else altogether. Commenting on a contemporary writer who expressed the received view that 'Aeneas indeed is a more amiable personage than Achilles; he seems meant for a perfect character', Blake wrote in the margin:

> Every body naturally hates a perfect character because they are all greater Villains than the imperfect, as Eneas is here shewn a worse man than Achilles in leaving Dido.   (K. 412)

The same author (Boyd, an early translator of Dante) had written that 'our feelings must tell us that Achilles carries his resentment to a savage length, a length where we cannot follow him'. But with this Blake disagrees:

> If Homer's merit was only in these Historical combinations & Moral sentiments he would be no better than Clarissa. (K. 411)

– and he expands this view:

> the grandest Poetry is Immoral, the Grandest characters Wicked, Very Satan – Capanius, Othello a murderer, Prometheus, Jupiter, Jehovah, Jesus a wine bibber. Cunning

& Morality are not Poetry but Philosophy; the Poet is Independent & Wicked; the Philosopher is Dependent & Good. (K. 412)

The 'eternal Realities as they Exist in the Human Imagination' are the scope of our humanity itself.

'True Art' in Blake's very specific sense of the word is whatever is inspired by the Imagination. It is in this sense spiritual irrespective of its association with temple or church or cult; although indeed all civilizations save our own (the first secular – that is to say materialist – civilization) art has everywhere been to be found, before all else, dedicated to the service of the gods. In declaring that 'all Deities reside in the human breast' Blake is by no means departing from this traditional use of art but, on the contrary, extending its scope. Whatever is the expression of mankind's deepest spiritual perceptions, at once our self-knowledge and our knowledge of the divine Ground, is 'true art' in Blake's sense, whether in the service of church or shrine or, like Chinese landscape-painting or the art of the Japanese No theatre, or the Quartets of Beethoven or those of T. S. Eliot, outside the context of any formal religious occasion. It is not the religions they serve which validate the arts: on the contrary, it is the quality of its imaginative vision that validates a religion. This is not to deny the truths of religion; on the contrary, they are true because grounded in Imagination. It was through Blake and in Blake's sense that Yeats came to declare himself for a religion of the arts with 'some help' from philosopher and theologian; for vision is primary, philosophy and theology being secondary elaboration only.

> The philosophy of the east taught the first principles of human perception: some nations held one principle for the origin, & some another: we of Israel taught that the Poetic Genius (as you now call it) was the first principle and all the others merely derivative, which was the cause of our despising the Priests & Philosophers of other countries, and prophecying that all Gods would prove to originate in ours & to be tributaries of the Poetic Genius. (K. 153)

In the historic Jesus Blake saw the fulfilment of the Jewish prophetic tradition. 'Jesus & his Apostles & Disciples were all

Artists', Blake declares; not, obviously, because they were painters, musicians or architects but because they lived at all times from the Imagination; for the highest of the arts is the living of life itself. The words of Jesus speak from the universal mind and therefore to the humanity all share; 'Christ addresses himself to the Man, not to his Reason.' (K. 774) He 'acted from impulse, not from rules.' (K. 158) – impulse, that is, from the God within.

A prophet is one who speaks for God; and for Blake God is within. He speaks from the Imagination. For Blake the prophetic and the poetic genius are the same thing; he writes of 'the Poetic Genius, which is everywhere call'd the Spirit of Prophecy' (K. 98) and invokes Milton, type of 'the inspired man':

'Let the Bard himself witness. Where hadst thou this terrible Song?'
The Bard replied: 'I am inspired! I know it is Truth! for I Sing
According to the inspiration of the Poetic Genius
Who is the eternal all-protecting Divine Humanity . . .'

(K. 495)

Blake writes of his own daily converse 'as man to man' with 'the Saviours's Kingdom', and he foretells a time when 'every man may converse with God & be a King & Priest in his own house.' (K. 389) There is a drawing by Blake of the Patriarch Enoch, surrounded by symbolic figures of poetry, painting and music, illustrating Jakob Boehme's Enochian Age; the age before the last, in which the divine knowledge is mediated through the arts. This depiction of the Enochian Age was for Blake doubtless a declaration of his own faith. In his series of illustrations to the Book of Job also the last plate shows Job and his children no longer studying books of the Law but playing on musical instruments and singing. In this series of illustrations to the Book of Job, Blake has represented the transformation of consciousness undergone by every man who from a religion of self-righteousness and the moral law comes to a perception of the God within. In the first of these plates we see Job and his wife reading to their assembled family the Book of the Law. Behind them on the Tree of Life hang, unused and unregarded, all kinds of instruments of music. In the last plate the Book of the Law has been forgotten and Job and his sons and daughters are all playing and singing: they are practising the religion of Imagination.

Blake himself claimed to have passed through a Last Judgment and he believed that others have done so; and he urges us all to press forward by imaginative vision to this supreme experience. He urges us to seek communion with 'those who are in eternity', the inspired artists and visionaries. These he has represented, in his composition on The Last Judgment, 'by some in a Cloud within the Rainbow that surrounds the Throne.' (K. 614) We can see them when we humble the reasoning and doubting selfhood, 'giving up all to Inspiration.'

Thus we see that the arts are for Blake of far greater import than they could (or should) ever be according to any materialist theory or within any materialist society. Yeats describes genius as 'a crisis that joins the buried self for certain moments to our trivial daily selves.' (*Autobiographies*; Hodos Chameleontos, ix) The Imagination is for the most part unconscious in us unless evoked by such means as music, architecture, poetry and the other arts; or indeed by such great beings as Jesus and the saints and sages of all religions who speak to the imagination rather than to the natural man. The artist's task is to bring back from that drowned world of the buried Self, which is alike in all human beings, images, themes which enable us to recollect, to renew our living connection with the state of being Blake calls Paradise; our native state since Imagination is the ground of our human existence itself.

In his poem *Milton* Blake sets forth his doctrine of inspiration. He calls the poet Milton – his type of 'the inspired man', – 'the awakener'; inspired himself, he awakens imaginative recollection in others and seeks to stir the 'sleepers' who life after life pass, in the words of Plotinus, 'from bed to bed, from sleep to sleep'. In 'the grandeur of inspiration' the poet puts off his human selfhood in order to speak from 'the true man', the poetic genius. It is because inspired poets, inspired musicians, speak not from their individual experience but from the mind that is common to all that their works have the power of awakening in us the universal visionary experience they mediate. Even the works of ages or civilizations remote from our own speak directly to us in this way – more directly than do contemporary works not grounded in the Imagination; for imagination is timeless. Blake makes his Milton answer those who ask,

. . . Where hadst thou this terrible Song?'
The Bard replied: 'I am Inspired! I know it is Truth! for I Sing
According to the inspiration of the Poetic Genius
Who is the eternal all-protecting Divine Humanity . . .'

(K. 495)

So understood the arts are the very food of our humanity. We share with the animal kingdom the need for bodily food, but man, as man, lives in another kingdom whose food is, as Jesus taught in the Gospel, the 'word of God'; words spoken from the Imagination to the imagination.

Blake loved Gothic art, its sculpture and architecture, and regarded our English Gothic churches as a true expression of the spiritual religion. These sublime expressions of the vision of another age continue to mediate that vision. Yet for the New Age 'stone churches' become superfluous, otherwise than as works of imagination. Like other great works of art these churches may serve as awakeners; but whatever function they owe merely to the religious organisation to which they nominally belong matters not at all. Blake's address 'To the Christians' which prefaces the fourth book of *Jerusalem* may be read as his manifesto for the new age:

> I know of no other Christianity and of no other Gospel than the liberty both of body & mind to exercise the Divine Arts of Imagination, Imagination, the real & eternal World of which this Vegetable Universe is but a faint shadow, & in which we shall live in our Eternal or Imaginative Bodies when these Vegetable Mortal Bodies are no more. The Apostles knew of no other Gospel. What were all their spiritual gifts? What is the Divine Spirit? Is the Holy Ghost any other than an Intellectual Fountain? What is the Harvest of the Gospel & its Labours? What is the Talent which it is a curse to hide? What are the Treasures of Heaven which we are to lay up for ourselves, are they any other than Mental Studies & performances? What are all the Gifts of the Gospel, are they not all Mental Gifts? Is God a Spirit who must be worshipped in Spirit & in Truth, and are not the Gifts of the Spirit Everything to Man? O ye Religious, discountenance every one among you who shall pretend to despise Art & Science!

And he concludes

> Let every Christian, as much as in him lies, engage himself
> openly & publicly before all the World in some Mental
> pursuit for the Building up of Jerusalem.   (K. 717)

5 Taylor, Blake and the English Romantic Movement

I belong to a generation which grew up in the unquestioned belief that every new development in human thought and in the arts comes about through breaking with the rules and restraints of the past, a revolutionary iconoclasm which 'frees' the mind of the artist for the production or reception of 'new ideas'. This assumption originated perhaps in a false analogy with science and the experimental method (we had not yet realized that science too can 'discover' only in accordance with its own presuppositions). In any case it suited our ignorance: freed from the burden of having to learn, we thought we could with more energy and single-mindedness create. But even the little history I had learned at school should have taught me better: had not the Italian Renaissance arisen out of a 'revival of learning' dormant for a thousand years? The phrase remained in my mind like an ungerminated seed, meaning nothing at all.

I have come to believe that every flowering of poetry and the other arts originates in a 'revival of learning'; not in 'originality' in the modern sense, but in a return to the origins, to first principles. I would now say that the learning which is 'revived' is always the same. Just as mathematics must in the future as in the past remain as the basis of calculations of a certain kind, without which buildings would not stand or aeroplanes fly, so do certain first principles of mind abide as the only ground of works of the imagination; the laws of mind, as of matter, are for ever established in the nature of things.

My generation even misapprehended the Romantic poets. Both those who admired and those who despised the Romantics took at its face value Wordsworth's claim to be using in his poetry the speech of common men. We were misled by the strong personal nature of Shelley's feelings into overlooking the beautifully articulated philosophic structure underlying his treatment of them; and by Blake's total and Keats's relative lack of schooling into supposing them as ignorant as ourselves. No sound scholar ever did or ever could have believed such things; but the disastrous modern vogue of 'criticism' (as opposed to scholarship) has continued to obscure the understanding of past works not immediately and obviously incomprehensible; even, perhaps especially, in the English Schools of the Universities. 'Criticism' is a good a pretext as iconoclastic avant-gardism for neglecting that 'revival of learning' which for so many besides myself has remained an empty phrase.

For as the Italian Renaissance drew its inspiration from the Platonic writings translated into Latin by Marsilio Ficino, so did the English Romantic Movement from those same works, translated for the first time into English by Thomas Taylor the Platonist. Such a statement must be an over-simplification; no great flowering of the arts could ever have only one cause; and yet I believe that the most powerful source of inspiration of the Romantic Movement was a revival of the Platonic philosophy. Why then have we heard so little of this? Principally because the revival of Platonism interrupted but did not stop the trend towards materialism at whose nadir we have perhaps arrived. A law might be formulated which is almost without exceptions: no critic will ever discover in the works he studies anything beyond his own presuppositions.

It takes a Platonist to recognise Platonism; and in spite of the conspiracy of silence which from first to last has involved Thomas Taylor and his remarkable writings and translations, the poets have discovered him with the same inevitability as the humanist critics have overlooked him. The works of 'Taylor the English Pagan' Coleridge names among the 'darling studies' of his schooldays; George Russell (Æ) called him 'the uncrowned King'; Yeats possessed some of his works, reissued by the Theosophical Society, or by John M. Watkins under the inspiration of that movement. I myself discovered Taylor when I was looking for the sources of William Blake; (*Blake and Tradition.* Bollingen Series 35 II. A. W. Mellon, Lectures on the Fine Arts, 1962 henceforth referred to as B.T.), and the more I read of his work, the more astonished I became that until the last few years

Taylor's name was almost unknown in England beyond the small circle I have indicated.

Yet he was a well-known figure in the London of his day. Isaac D'Israeli included him in his series of *English Publick Characters for 1792*. He lent himself to satire, and on the title-page of his two-volume translation of Proclus' *Commentaries on Euclid* he himself quotes from Isaac D'Israeli's *Curiosities of Literature*: 'Mr. T. Taylor, the Platonic Philosopher and *the modern Plethon*, consonant to that philosophy, professes Polytheism'. His intention was to shock, and he was successful; according to rumour, he sacrificed a bull to Zeus in his house at Walworth (a difficult undertaking one would think) and worshipped Apollo with equally appropriate rites. D'Israeli put him in his novel *Vaurien*, and William Blake in his *Island on the Moon*, where he appears as 'Sipsop the Pythagorean', arguing that Giotto is of no importance because he was not an ancient Greek. In Thomas Love Peacock's *Melincourt*, Taylor is 'Mr. Mystic'. Peacock – whom Taylor called 'Greeky-peeky' was a regular visitor; and may have taken his friend Shelley to call on the Platonist. (*Thomas Taylor the Platonist* Ed. by Kathleen Raine and George Mills Harper, Bollingen Series p. 88 henceforth referred to as R. & H.)

Taylor was the son of a non-conformist father, who sent him to St Paul's school, and intended him for Aberdeen University; Oxford and Cambridge at that time were closed to dissenters. But Taylor made instead a rash early marriage – a very happy one, apparently – and did not go to any university. He worked hard in a number of ill-paid posts, but was presently, through the patronage of the picturesque and Liberal Charles, Eleventh Duke of Norfolk, made Assistant Secretary to the Society of Arts and Sciences in the Adelphi. The Duke remained Taylor's patron after he left the Society to devote himself to his Platonic studies, and subscribed to the whole edition of his Plato – the first translation of the whole of Plato's works into English. Among his friends were George Cumberland; Mary Wollstonecraft, who was for a time a lodger with the Taylors; Flaxman, at whose house he gave a series of twelve lectures on the Platonic philosophy. The French Platonist, the Liberal Marquis de Valady, guillotined during the Terror, also stayed with Taylor during his residence in England. His portrait was painted by Sir Thomas Lawrence (the original is in Ottawa, a copy at the National Portrait Gallery in London). And yet there has been a resolute determination, from the first reviews of his works ever written, to consign Taylor to oblivion.

Whatever the faults of Taylor's scholarship or of his English style it is not for these he was hated. But he was guilty of two unforgivable violations of the unwritten law: he trespassed upon a field which a number of Dons regarded as their preserve and he took seriously the writings of the Platonic philosophers. He was a professed follower of 'a theology the most venerable of all others for its antiquity, and' – this above all – 'the most admirable for its excellence and reality.' In 1787 a little anonymous book of some fifty pages appeared, which was to set in train a revolution in poetry and the arts: *An Essay on the Beautiful*, a paraphrased translation from the Greek of Plotinus (Ennead, 1. 6.). Taylor's only previous work had been *A New Method of Reasoning in Geometry* (1780) published when the author was twenty-one; he later wrote that he came to study Greek philosophy first through mathematics. *On the Beautiful* went into a second edition in 1792, and was reissued in 1895 by the Theosophical Society. Had Taylor been one of those 'pendants' and 'verbal critics' with whom he carried on a lifelong war, nobody would have troubled about him; but his object was militant: 'to diffuse the salutary light of genuine philosophy.' His two-volume *Commentaries on Euclid* bears on its title-page (besides the profession of polytheism) a dedication *To the Sacred Majesty of Truth*. The early 1790s were years of revolution; on the throne of Paris sat the Goddess Reason; and Taylor's patron the Eleventh Duke of Norfolk was banished for a time from public life for proposing the toast of another and more successful pretender to the English throne than Taylor's Sacred Majesty: 'To our Sovereign, The People.' Such was the world in which Taylor raised the banner of Plotinus:

> With respect to true philosophy, you must be sensible that all modern sects are in a state of barbarous ignorance: for Materialism, and its attendant Sensuality, have darkened the eyes of the *many*, with the mists of error; and are continually strengthening their corporeal tie. And can any thing more effectually dissipate this increasing gloom than dis-

courses composed by so sublime a genius, pregnant with the most profound conceptions, and everywhere full of intellectual light? Can any thing so thoroughly destroy the phantom of false enthusiasm, as establishing the real object of the true? Let us then boldly enlist ourselves under the banner of Plotinus, and, by his assistance, vigorously repel the encroachments of error, plunge her dominions into the abyss of forgetfulness, and disperse the darkness of her baneful night. For, indeed, there never was a period which required so much philosophic exertion; or such vehement contention from the lovers of Truth. On all sides, nothing of philosophy remains but the name, and this is become the subject of the vilest prostitution: since it is not only engrossed by the Naturalist, Chemist and Anatomist, but is usurped by the Mechanic, in every trifling invention, and made subservient to the lucre of traffic and merchandize. There cannot surely be a greater proof of the degeneracy of the times than so unparalleled a degradation, and so barbarous a perversion of terms . . . Rise, then, my friends, and the victory will be ours. The foe is indeed numerous, but, at the same time, feeble: and the weapons of truth, in the hands of vigorous union, descend with irresistable force, and are fatal wherever they fall. (R. & H. p. 159)

Taylor boldly engaged himself in a battle on two fronts. In his profession of 'the Creed of the Platonic Philosopher' he declared himself, in no uncertain terms, an anti-Christian. Blake in the name of Christianity damned the clergy of the late eighteenth century as thoroughly as did Taylor in the name of Plotinus; but whatever may be thought of the spirituality of the clergy of that time, there is possibly even less to be said for their contribution to Classical studies. *The Edinburgh Review*, in a scathing denunciation of Taylor's translation of the complete works of Plato in 1804 was compelled to admit that

. . . preposterous share of time, labour and esteem . . . bestowed upon the comparatively unimportant business of prosody (regarded as a cardinal point in English Education) is the cause of the rarity, even among the most celebrated scholars in England, of anything like a familiar acquaintance with the orators, the philosophers and the historians of Greece.

To the protestant clergymen who at that time made up the academic world, the Platonic theology would in any case have been extremely distasteful, and Taylor's professions of Platonism as outrageous as was Shelley's Hellenistic atheism a generation later, to the Master and Fellows of University College, Oxford. As a man with nothing to lose Taylor had no fear of speaking his mind about the pedant

> who has spent the prime of his life, and consumed the vigour of his understanding in verbal criticism and grammatical trifles . . . Whoever reads the lives of the ancient Heroes of Philosophy, must be convinced that they studied things more than words, and that Truth alone was the ultimate object of their search.

It is not surprising that several of Taylor's works were published anonymously, or under fictitious imprints; and that the whole edition of Plato was kept by the Duke of Norfolk under lock and key in his library; Plato's in those days was a dangerous creed to profess.

There were plenty of people at the turn of the eighteenth century who would have been willing to applaud in the name of the Goddess Reason Taylor's castigations of the 'black coated gentlemen' of Oxford; but his contempt for the clergy was exceeded only by his contempt for the mechanistic philosophers. The ideas of Bacon, Newton and Locke he regarded as far more dangerous than the purely negative stupidity of the bishops and dons of Oxford. To Taylor's contemporaries it must have seemed mere arrogance to declare that Newton, though a good mathematician, was no philosopher; or that 'the conceptions of the experimental philosopher who expects to find truth in the labyrinths of matter, are not much more elevated than those of the vulgar'; and that the thought of Bacon and Locke would sooner or later perish with 'the variety of other self-taught systems which, like nocturnal meteors, blaze for a while, then vanish in obscurity.' Of Bacon and Locke he wrote the former of these is celebrated for having destroyed the jargon of the schoolmen, and brought experimental enquiries into repute; and for attempting to investigate causes through the immensity of particular effects. Hence, he fondly expected, by experiment piled on experiment, to reach the principle of the universe . . . the later of these, Mr. Locke, is applauded for having, without assistance from the ancients, explained the nature, and exhibited the genuine theory of human understanding.

Locke had laid the foundation of Behaviourism:

> According to Mr. Locke, the soul is a mere rasa tabula, an empty recipient, a mechanical blank. According to Plato she is an ever-written tablet, a plentitude of forms, a vital intellectual energy.

Taylor wished to see a restoration of the Platonic theology which he held to be the true religion; or, more exactly, as a notable manifestation of 'the one universal and unanimous tradition':

> As to the philosophy, by whose assistance these mysteries are developed, it is coeval with the universe itself; and however its continuity may be broken by opposing systems, it will make its appearance at different periods of time, as long as the sun himself shall continue to illuminate the world. It has, indeed, and may hereafter, be violently assaulted by delusive opinions; but the opposition will be just as imbecil as that of the waves of the sea against a temple built on a rock, which majestically pours them back, 'Broken and vanquish'd foaming to the main. (*Dissertation on the Eleusinian and Bacchic Mysteries*)

Taylor, like Blake, worked in defiance of the unwritten censorship of received opinion to restore a great body of excluded knowledge of no mean order.

Who then were the 'lovers of truth' who responded when Taylor raised the standard of Plotinus? One certainly was William Blake. Confirmation of the acquaintance between Blake and Thomas Taylor has been found by Dr James King of Toronto

University, who in the papers of William Meredith, an architect and friend of Taylor, discovered an amusing description, characteristic of both men, of Taylor teaching Blake a Theorem from the Elements of Euclid:

> Wednesday, Decr. 30, 1829 [Note that this is the date of the diary entry, not of the event described] T. Taylor gave Blake, the artist, some lessons on mathematics & got as far as the 5th proposition which proves that ye two angles at base of an isosceles triangle must be equal. Taylor was going thro the demonstration, but was interrupted by Blake exclaiming 'ah never mind that – what's the use of going to prove it. Why I see with my eyes that it is so, & do not require any proof to make it clearer. (The Meredith Family, Thomas Taylor, and William Blake. By James King, *Studies in Romanticism* XI, Spring 1972 No. 2)

Taylor's two-volume edition of Proclus' *Commentaries on Euclid* contains several essays, including *A History of the Restoration of the Platonic theology by the Later Platonists*, which contains a translation of the whole of Porphyry's *De Antro Nympharum*. These essays were in all probability the substance of the series of lectures on Platonism which Taylor gave at the house of 'Flaxman, the Statuary' who played so important a part in the Greek Revival in the field of the visual arts. Flaxman invited for Taylor's lectures a distinguished audience, which included Romney; and which certainly must have included, amongst those whose names were not important enough to mention, Flaxman's close friend and fellow Swedenborgian, William Blake. These lectures must have been given before Flaxman and his wife went to Italy in the year 1787, there to remain for seven years. Flaxman was a year older than Taylor and a year younger than Blake, who was born in 1757; all three were in their early thirties at the time, and at the outset of their careers. These, I believe, with George Cumberland, (friend of Taylor and of Blake and one of the founders of the National Gallery) were the first of the 'Men of the New Age' (Blake's phrase) to be fired by Taylor's enthusiasm for the Platonic philosophy.

The Greek revival had already begun in the visual arts; Stuart and Revett, the draftsman and architect, visited Ionia and Athens in the 1760s and their remarkable plans and drawings of Greek architecture and sculpture were published in a series of volumes extending into the nineteenth century. Few Englishmen had as yet visited Greece; but works of Greek and Graeco–Roman sculpture and ceramics had for some time been making their way to England. One of the first works to create a widespread excitement was the Barberini vase (later to become the Portland Vase) brought back in 1784 by Sir William Hamilton, husband of Nelson's (and Romney's) Emma. The world, then as now, was a small one: it was Flaxman who in his enthusiasm for Sir William Hamilton's vase persuaded his employer Josiah Wedgwood to make his famous replicas, which were in due course exhibited in London at the Wedgwood showrooms in 1790. The Wedgwoods' friend Erasmus Darwin included in his *Botanic Garden* a set of engravings of the vase, and an essay explaining its emblems as depictions of the Eleusinian Mysteries; the engravings were made by Blake; and Taylor published in 1790 or 1791 his own brilliant *Dissertation on the Mysteries of Eleusis and Dionysus*.

The Eleusinian Mysteries were in vogue in the early 1790s; and Taylor's book must have been read by many who at the time were under the spell of the Portland Vase and the Wedgwood replicas.

It was Taylor who provided the philosophic foundations of the Greek revival. Its visual aspects, from the Elgin Marbles, beloved by Keats, to Flaxman's famous illustrations of Homer and Hesiod, and the well-known intaglios he and others made for the Wedgwoods, have very understandably overshadowed other aspects of that transformation of consciousness which took place in all the arts at the end of the eighteenth century. Blake no less than Flaxman came under the influence of the Greek revival, though less obviously, and less visually; and his young disciples, Palmer, Richmond, Calvert and Finch called themselves, a generation later, 'the Shoreham Ancients' – echoing still Taylor's call to the 'lovers of Truth' to abandon the delusive opinions of 'the moderns' for the philosophic wisdom of 'the ancients'. In a letter from Palmer written in 1838, when the painter was on his honeymoon in Italy, he declares himself a Platonist:

Blessed also will be the mind that is imbued with Plato –
would that mine were so! – the very antithesis of the
literary impudence, dandyism and materialism with which
most of our modern periodicals tend imperceptibly to imbue
the mind. If I am ever to open a book again and not to
'live a fool and die a brute', may I open once more the divine
leaves of Plato in some happy Grove Street evening with you
and dear Anny [Palmer's wife] by my fireside – but it is
too good to be hoped for in this world except with Euripides
in his Cave; too deep to hear the rumbling of her rubbish
carts. (*Samuel Palmer's Honeymoon.* Edward Malins,
1968.)

Is this still a remote echo of Taylor's call to the banner of
Plotinus? It is almost certain that the 'divine leaves of Plato'
would have been Taylor's translation rather than the volumes
published by Floyer Sydenham whose work, left incomplete at
the time of his death, the young Taylor had continued. Sydenham,
the first to undertake an English translation of Plato, died of
poverty and neglect, in a debtor's prison.

It is in Blake's writings that we first meet with the new ideas
of Taylor's revival of learning. Blake later reacted against Plato
and 'the Greek and Roman slaves of the sword' and quite possibly quarrelled with Taylor, who may well have been the
'antique borer' to whom he referred in a letter to their mutual
friend George Cumberland some years later; but during the 1790s
he was writing that 'the purpose for which alone I live is to
restore the lost art of the Greeks.' His references to Plato and
Socrates throughout his life are made in a spirit of almost
brotherly intimacy, whether Blake is agreeing or disagreeing with
them; and in his old age he had become, so Palmer says, 'a
Platonist in politics'. One of Blake's last paintings, the Arlington
Court tempera provisionally entitled *The Sea of Time and Space*
(1821) is an illustration of Porphyry's *Cave of the Nymphs*,
included by Taylor in one of his earliest works, *On the Restoration of the Platonic Theology by the Latter Platonists*, included
in the second volume of Proclus' *Commentaries on Euclid*, (1789).
But the greatest impact upon Blake of the Platonic philosophy
was the first – between 1787 and 1804. It was during those years
that each successive publication by Taylor was to find its immedi-

ate echo in Blake's writings. The two poems *The Little Girl Lost* and *The Little Girl Found* reflect the account of the Eleusinian Mysteries given in Taylor's *Dissertation on the Mysteries of Eleusis and Dionysus* (1790), while the *Book of Thel* reflects his translation of Plotinus *On the Beautiful* (1804).

As each new volume of Taylor's *Works* appeared, so do we find its traces in the contemporaneous works of Blake.

One of Blake's earliest works, the three tractates on Natural Religion declares in its title – *All Religions are One* – his adherence, at that time, not so much to Christianity as to the *sophia perennis*. These tractates discuss the question of the nature of 'the true man'; he is answering Locke, who held the materialist view that 'Naturally man is a natural organ subject to sense'; but the phrase itself, 'the true man', as well as Blake's arguments, Taylor had used and developed in his own philosophic objections to the theories of Locke, in his *Dissertation on the Platonic Doctrine of Ideas* – which doctrine (or its equivalent) is the only possible answer to Locke. 'The true man, both according to Aristotle and Plato, is intellect' – so Taylor reaffirms the traditional premise of every ancient philosophy: mind, not matter, is the primary reality of the universe. It seems more likely that Taylor, who was a mathematician and a metaphysician engaged in works on the theory of ideas, first formulated the philosophic objections to Bacon and Locke than that Blake thought of them for himself. Taylor's argument for the Platonic view of intellect as the substantial reality and 'the true man' is far more minutely argued than in Blake's powerful aphorisms, which read, to any one familiar with both, like an impassioned summary of Taylor's work; as I believe they are. As to 'the true man' Blake goes one better than Taylor – or perhaps Plato – saying that the true man is neither (as Locke supposed) 'a natural organ' nor, as Taylor says, 'intellect', but 'the poetic genius'. By this he means the prophetic spirit of Israel, which transcends reason. In his later works he is still more explicit, and in the phrase 'Jesus the Imagination', dissociates himself from Taylor's anti-Christian Platonism; yet Blake's use of the word 'imagination' in this sense is itself Platonic; 'intellect', the more usual translation of *nous*, signifies the divine mind or supra-sensible intelligible world; the Platonic term has not the modern connotation of rationalism, but is akin to the Christian Logos, as being the Cosmic intellect and that in man which knows truth by immediate perception. In his definition of 'the true man' Blake was the first of the Romantic poets to affirm that supremacy of the Imagination which is their common creed.

Taylor and Blake were both engaged in making their attack upon the very root of the irreconcilable difference between the materialist and the Platonic view of man. If we turn to a more recent poet upon whose shelves also stood works of Thomas Taylor, we find Yeats making precisely the same impassioned affirmation of the active nature of the soul, as against Locke's doctrine of its passivity, since developed into the theory of Behaviourism, and the practice of 'brain-washing'. Yeats wrote in his Introduction to the *Oxford Book of Modern Verse*,

> The mischief began at the end of the seventeenth century when man became passive before a mechanized nature; that lasted down to our own day with the exception of a brief period between Smart's *Song to David* and the death of Byron, wherein imprisoned man beat upon the door.

Plotinus' tractate *On the Beautiful* contains the essence of the Platonic (or Neo-Platonic) aesthetics, which through Coleridge and through Shelley's *Defence of Poetry* was to become the canon of the Romantic aesthetic doctrine. When in 1908 Mackenna, in his turn, published his own translation of this seminal and beautiful work, he prefaced it with a line from a Renaissance Platonist, Spenser: 'For Soul is Form and doth the Body make' – Plotinus' principle of the precedence of wholes over parts, of informing idea over the material medium, applied specifically to works of art. Coleridge's definition of beauty, as he gives it in his chapter *On the Principles of Genial Criticism* in the *Biographia Literaria* is that of Plotinus: "participation in a forming-idea"; a conception he refers back to Pythagoras: "the reduction of the many to the one", or again "the subjection of matter to spirit, so as to be transformed into a symbol"; that is to say, the material embodiment in its turn suggests and evokes the spiritual essence which informs it. "I would that the readers for whom alone I write", Coleridge continues, "had Raphael's Galatea, or his School of Athens before them!" – acknowledging, in such examples, that the Renaissance artists exemplified in their work these Platonic definitions of the beautiful.' He then breaks into a panegyric on

> Plotinus, a name venerable even to religion with the great Cosmus, Lorenzo de Medici, Ficinus, Politian, Leonardo da Vinci and Michael Angelo, but now known only as a name to the majority even of our most learned Scholars! Plotinus, difficult indeed, but under a rough and austere rind concealing fruit worthy of paradise . . .

He then goes on to quote (in Greek) a passage from *Ennead* 1. 6 of *On the Beautiful* which Taylor had translated.

> When, therefore, sense beholds the form in bodies at strife with matter, binding and vanquishing its contrary nature, and sees form gracefully shining forth in other forms, it collects together the scattered whole, and introduces it to itself, and to the indivisible form within; and renders it consonant, congruous and friendly to its own intimate form.

To this Coleridge says that a passage in his own poem, the 'Ode to Dejection', is an approximation; the underlinings are Coleridge's own:

> O lady! we *receive* but what we *give*
> And in *our* life alone doth nature live!
> Ours is her wedding-garment, ours her shroud!
> And would we ought behold of higher worth
> Than that inanimate cold world allow'd
> To the poor, loveless, ever-anxious crowd:
> Ah! from the soul itself must issue forth
> A light, a glory, a fair luminous cloud, enveloping the earth!
> And from the soul itself must there be sent
> A sweet and powerful voice of its own birth
> Of all sweet sounds the life and element!

The passage continues to expand this idea in a series of beautiful images from nature; which serve to reflect, the poet says,

> This beautiful, this beauty-making power.

There has been a movement in our own time among poets away from the conception of beauty, which to philosophers and artists within the Platonic tradition is of the very essence of art. The realists – who tend to be influenced by the Marxist or some other form of materialist philosophy – would justify the dullness or formless vulgarity of their depictions on the grounds of truth to the fact of observation. A follower of the Platonic tradition would see in this a capitulation of the spirit, in which resides the 'beauty-making power', to that 'mechanized nature' of which Yeats speaks, and whose earlier exponent, Locke, was challenged with such energy by Blake and Taylor. Nature has not ceased to be beautiful; never, according to Blake, was beautiful, except insofar as nature can reflect whatever, in Coleridge's words, issues forth from the soul. It is the poets who have renounced the faculty by which alone the poetic function to which they pretend belongs to them. Not indeed all; the last poem Edwin Muir wrote acknowledges:

> That Plato's is the truest poetry
> And that these shadows
> Are cast by the true.

May we not say that the view of the passive nature of mind is inimical to, perhaps incompatible with, the creation of works of art? If as Shelley stated, poetry is the language of imagination, the Platonic view of intellect as an active agent, and Blake's belief that the true man is imagination itself, 'the poetic genius', is surely implicit. If Locke's view were true what would become of Coleridge's 'esemplastic power',

> My shaping spirit of imagination

It is true that Coleridge could and did read the Greek authors in the original Greek, as did Shelley, though not Blake or Keats or even (probably) Wordsworth; but how far had Coleridge's school-boy enthusiasm, which he describes in his *Biographia*, for the writings of Taylor, the English Pagan, prepared the way for his later and mature thought on the nature of the imagination and of the poetic art? The wave of Platonic enthusiasm of which Coleridge is perhaps the greatest figure, was set in motion by Taylor.

To trace the influence of Plotinus alone through Coleridge's work would probably demand a book; Plato and Plotinus were for him the supreme philosophers; on one occasion he added the name of Proclus whose Platonic commentaries Taylor had translated and published in 1810. For doing so Taylor had been mocked and abused at the time; for many reviewers who would not have dared to attack Plato felt that they could with impunity ridicule Proclus, whose name was scarcely known. Thus the Edinburgh Review, in an article attacking Taylor's Plato, wrote:

> He has not translated Plato, he has travestied him in the most abominable manner. He has not elucidated him, but covered him over with impenetrable darkness.

How so? By adding, by way of notes, Proclus' commentaries:

> In the character of commentator Mr. Taylor has scarcely done anything, or indeed professed to do anything, but to fasten upon Plato the reveries of Proclus, and of other philosophers of the Alexandrian school.

That such arrogant ignorance could pass itself off as serious judgment seems almost incredible; but the philistine attitude which lies behind such vulgar journalism is expressed more openly by Horace Walpole in a private letter:

> I guess that the religion this new apostle recommends is not belief in the pantheon of the Pagan divinities, but the creed of the philosophers who really did not believe in their idols, but whose metaphysics were frequently as absurd; and yet this half-witted Taylor prefers them to Bacon and Locke, who were almost the first philosophers who introduced common sense into their writings and were as clear as Plato was unintelligible – because he did not understand himself.

Walpole, in a letter to a lady, did not attempt to disguise the truth: the real objection of the Enlightenment was to Plato himself; whose philosophy was, quite simply, incomprehensible within their terms of reference. Without wishing to detract from

Coleridge's originality as a philosopher of poetry, it must be said, again, that Taylor had prepared the way for Coleridge's reversal of the judgment of Walpole and the Edinburgh reviewer, who declared that

> the ravings of Jacob Boehme are not a more abominable misrepresentation of the New Testament than the commentaries of Proclus and Company of the writings of Plato

(Boehme too was a key figure in the Romantic Revival, acknowledged as such by Coleridge as well as Blake.) In the margin of his copy of Taylor's Proclus, Coleridge wrote:

> Let a prepared scholar attentively peruse Chapter VI Book I . . . if possible in the original Greek, and the result in his mind will inform him, whether Nature has intended him for metaphysical Research. If I have any conception of Sublimity as arising from a majestic vision of tranquil Truth, it will be found in this Chapter.

What to Coleridge was 'beautiful and orderly' was to Walpole 'nonsense' and to the Edinburgh Review 'impenetrable darkness.' When we read that a philosopher is unintelligible, we must ask, 'to whom?'

The essential resemblance and sympathy of ideas between Blake and Coleridge arises, I believe, from their common debt (through Taylor, partially in the case of Coleridge, and wholly in the case of Blake) to the Platonic philosophers. Coleridge acknowledges his sources; Blake merely makes use of them. They are easily discovered, because Blake had an exact verbal memory and words and even phrases appear in his writings, lifted entire from the authors from whom he borrowed; just as in his designs details may be traced to works of visual art which he had studied with the same minute attention. Many passages in his prose and verse writings prove his indebtedness to Plotinus' *On the Beautiful*, upon which his own Platonic theory of art (as expressed, especially, in his poem *Milton*) is founded. But more interesting is the way in which he would seize upon and personify some illustrative image, or even from a philosophic abstraction make a myth or

symbolic episode. Several of these he took from *On the Beautiful.*
The Book of Thel (1789) is, like the tractates *On Natural*
Religion, concerned with the nature of 'the true man'; Thel is the
soul who mistakes the shadow for the substance, the materialist
fallacy. Her watery flowing landscape, of 'shadows in the water',
'reflection in a glass', is a symbolic world constructed from those
very images Plotinus uses to illustrate his theme of the soul
mistaking its reflection in matter (the body) for substantial
reality:

> . . . the forms which appear in matter are . . . shadows falling
> upon shadow, as in a mirror, where the position of a thing
> is different from its real situation . . . but the things which
> enter and depart from matter are nothing but imitations of
> being, and semblances.

In *Visions of the Daughters of Albion* (1793) the landscape is
again Platonic, a 'cave' by the shore of the 'sea' of material
existence, 'the dark ocean of corporeal life', according to a phrase
Taylor used in a note to *On the Beautiful*. In this poem Blake
takes up another theme of Plotinus, in the same work, the radical
innocence of the soul. Oothoon, the figure who in this poem
represents the soul, has been ravished by Bromion; and her lover
Theotormon, blinded by the materialist view of virtue, cannot
believe her pure. Oothoon 'as the clear spring, mudded with the
feet of beasts, grows pure & smiles.' The doctrine is that of
Plotinus, who says that the soul.

> becoming impure, and being on all sides snatched in the
> unceasing whirl of sensible forms, is covered wholly with
> corporeal stains . . . just as the pristine beauty of the most
> lovely form would be destroyed by its total immersion in
> mire and clay.

But the deformity arises from . . .

> the accession of some foreign nature. If such a one desire
> to recover his former beauty, it is necessary to cleanse the
> infected parts, and thus by a thorough purgation to resume
> his original form . . . As the gold is deformed by the
> adherence to earthly clods, which are no sooner removed
> than the gold shines forth.

In *Milton* Blake returns to the theme in the great concluding pages of the poem which begin with the lines:

To cleanse the Face of my Spirit by Self-examination,
To bathe in the Waters of Life, to wash off the Not Human . . .

(K. 533)

Theotormon cannot believe in the soul's radical innocence, and:

. . . sits
Upon the margin'd ocean *conversing with shadows dire.*

(K. 195)

Again the passage from which the image is taken is easy to recognise:

Hence as Narcissus, by catching at the shadow, merged himself in the stream, and disappeared, so he who is captivated by beautiful bodies, and does not depart from their embrace, is precipitated, not with his body, but with his soul, into a darkness profound and horrid to intellect, through which, becoming blind both here and in Hades, *he converses with nothing but shadows.*

So often in his later work does Blake return to the images and themes of *On the Beautiful* that I would even suggest that his apparently simple early poem *The Little Boy Lost* (before 1789) may reflect the impact of Taylor's work in its images, and Blake's Little Boy, who strays into the darkness of materialism, is to the figure of Narcissus what his *Little Girl Lost* is to the *Kore* of the Eleusinian Mysteries. The Little Boy's pursuit of the phantom is Plotinus' pursuit of the 'nonentity' matter, as quoted by Taylor in a note to *On the Beautiful*:

. . . a phantom, neither abiding, nor yet able to fly away: capable of no one denomination, and possessing no power from intellect; but constituted in the defect, a shade as it were of all real being. Hence, too, in each of our vanishing appellations it eludes our search . . . and the apparent being which we meet with in its image, is non-being, and as it were a flying mockery.

So for Blake's Little Boy:

The mire was deep, the child did weep,
And away the vapour flew.

One of the most interesting figures in Blake's mythology – Enion – appears to be, quite simply, a personification of Plotinus' 'flying mockery', matter, as a philosophic *non-ens*; her counter-part is Tharmas, called in certain passages 'the eternal man' – the 'true man' of Blake's and Taylor's early writings – intellect, with-out whose 'illuminations' matter remains a formless *non-ens*. The name Tharmas appears to be taken from a myth in the *Hermetica* which describes the True Man's fall into the sea of matter, lured down by a female figure who personifies that principle. The pass-age from Plotinus from which we have already quoted above evidently provided Blake not only with the figure of Enion (whose very name suggests the Platonic *non-ens*) but also the episodes of her flight and the pursuit of the enamoured Tharmas:

> Since matter is neither soul nor intellect, nor life, nor form, nor reason, nor bound, but a certain indefiniteness; nor yet capacity, for what can it produce? Since it is foreign from all these, it cannot merit the appellation of being, but is deservedly called non-entity . . . a mere shadow and imagina-tion of bulk, and the desire of subsistence: abiding without station, of itself invisible, and avoiding the desire of him who wishes to perceive its nature. Hence, when no-one perceives it, it is then in a manner present: but cannot be viewed by him who strives intently to behold it. (Enneads III. 6. 7 R. & H. p. 147.)

This definition would satisfy a modern scientist more easily than the mechanistic philosophers of the eighteenth century; Blake understood the force of the argument about matter and appearances; and the force of the episode of Enion and Tharmas in *Vala* becomes clear only when we have identified these figures as the Platonic contraries of Intellect and Matter. Enion is said to wander 'on the margin of non-entity'. In accordance with her character as ensnaring matter (for Plotinus the only principle of evil), and with the materialist age of which her myth is an expres-sion, she tries to assert her supremacy over Tharmas, by ensnaring him in her 'filmy woof' and drowning him, like Narcissus, in the sea of *hyle*. Her success is followed by her repentance; for she discovers that, without the 'irradiation of intellect' she is in danger of being consumed away; and pleads:

> . . . tho' I have sinned, tho' I have rebell'd
> Make me not like the things forgotten as they had not been.

The 'sin' and 'rebellion' of Enion suggest a passage from Plotinus'
On the Descent of the Soul, published by Taylor in *Five Books
of Plotinus* (1794):

> Matter, indeed, being present, with wanton importunity,
> affects, and desires, as it were, to penetrate into the inward
> recesses of the soul. Matter, therefore, opposing herself to
> soul, is illustrated by its divine light, yet is incapable of
> receiving that by which it is illustrated, because through
> its depravity, it is incapable of beholding a nature so pure
> and divine.

She begs to be permitted to remain near Tharmas, her 'loved
terror' because although she 'cannot sustain the irradiations of
soul', yet her very existence depends upon his presence; for, as
Plotinus says, 'reason and form entering the obscure involutions
of matter, irradiates and forms its dark and formless nature':

I am almost Extinct & soon shall be a shadow in Oblivion
Unless some way can be found that I may look upon thee and live,
Hide me in some shadowy semblance. . . .

– so she pleads to be 'illustrated' and 'irradiated' by that same
divine light of the soul which had inspired Coleridge to write:

And in our life alone does Nature live

– in a poem itself inspired, as he tells us, by Plotinus.

Both Enion and the female figure in *A Mental Traveller* to
whom she corresponds symbolically, hide from the pursuing
intellectual principle in the 'labyrinths' of matter – Plotinus'
'obscure involutions.' Taylor uses the word in this sense in
several contexts, including the Introduction to *On the Beautiful*:

> . . . to pursue matter, through its infinite divisions, and
> wander in its dark labyrinths, is the employment of the
> philosophy in vogue.

He is referring, of course, to Bacon, who had used the word
labyrinth in this sense.

Blake never missed an occasion to create, from an all but abstract word, phrase, or concept, a symbolic landscape as overwhelming as that of dream, concrete, and unmistakably Blakean.

Coleridge, like Blake, was a mythological poet and a symbolist; Wordsworth was not, nor was he, like Coleridge, a scholar by nature. Perhaps it was Coleridge who fired Wordsworth with his own enthusiasm for Plotinus; for it is certain that he too had read some of Taylor's translations. The theology of the *Ode on the Intimation of Immortality* is, like Blake's, Platonic and not Christian, for Wordsworth too supposes the pre-existence of the soul.

The symbol of 'life's star' comes from Plato's account of the descent of souls (as stars) into generation, given in the Tenth Book of *The Republic*. The phrase 'the Inward Eye', so familiar to readers of Wordsworth's *The Daffodils* is Platonic; the phrase appears on p. 41 of *On the Beautiful*; it is 'the purer eye within', by which we behold 'a beauty not visible to the corporeal eye, but alone manifest to the brighter eye of the soul' – a theme Plotinus discusses at length in this tractate.

One of Taylor's richest works is his paraphrased translation of *Five Books of Plotinus*; of these, one is *On the Descent of the Soul*, and from it Blake seems to have taken the essence of his own theology of the descent and return of souls between the 'sleep' or 'death' of generation and the soul's native country. Blake describes the 'sleep' or 'death' of the generated soul, 'To rise from generation free', returning to its native country; a descent and return made perhaps many times. Another is *On Felicity*; and here we meet the traces of Wordsworth. *On Felicity* opens with a discussion of the nature of happiness; Plotinus is arguing a proposition which must have pleased Wordsworth, that 'to live according to nature is to live well'; and he begins by saying that 'living well belongs to other animals as well as man' and he instances the birds, whose song suggests that they live according to nature and

> . . . possess a desirable life. But if we constitute felicity as a certain end, which is something extreme in the appetite of nature, in this way all animals will be happy when they arrive at this extreme, and which, when obtained, Nature in them makes a stop, as having accomplished the whole of

their existence, and filled it with all that is wanting from beginning to end.

He goes on to ask whether plants, too, may enjoy felicity, 'whose slender existence arrives at its proper term', and admits that 'some may allow felicity to plants, since life is present even to these.' He devotes several pages to discussing the nature of felicity in its special relationship to animals and plants. Wordsworth's *Lines Written in Early Spring* is virtually a paraphrase of Plotinus' argument. He begins, as Plotinus does, with the birds, and goes on to plants; while implicit in the whole poem is the belief that to 'live according to nature' is the source of happiness for man no less than for these:

> Through primrose tufts, in that sweet bower,
> The periwinkle trail'd its wreaths;
> And 'tis my faith that every flower
> Enjoys the air it breathes.
>
> The birds around me hopp'd and play'd
> Their thoughts I cannot measure –
> But the least motion which they made
> It seem'd a thrill of pleasure.
>
> The budding twigs spread out their fan
> To catch the breezy air;
> And I must think, do what I can,
> That there was pleasure there.

There is in the volume which contains Taylor's paraphrase translation *On Felicity*, Plotinus' *On Nature, Contemplation and the One*; and a good case could be made to show that 'nature', in the special sense in which Wordsworth uses the word, is an idea taken from Plotinus.

The most radical change which came about in English poetry as a direct result, as it would seem, of Thomas Taylor's translations and commentaries, was the new use made by the Romantic poets of the symbolic language of mythology. Emerson (who with Bronson Alcott spread Taylor's fame in America at a time when in England he was for the most part neglected) called the English Pagan 'the best feeder of poets since Milton'; and if so, it was principally in his restoration to mythological discourse of some semblance of its true meaning and richness of connotation after some two centuries of incomprehension. Myths can, in their very nature, be read upon several levels; indeed exist in order to establish relations between the multiple planes of being. At the same time myths cannot be made to mean anything we please. There has been a recent fashion among psychologists, for example, to borrow the myths of Oedipus or the Marriage of Cupid and Psyche for purposes of their own which, however admirable in themselves, are remote from the meanings which these figures and stories existed to communicate within the tradition and culture to which they properly belong. These personal interpretations can only destroy the themes which are thus detached from their context. Only within the context of a whole culture can myths be properly understood. It may be said that the Alexandrian philosophers made use of the Greek myths in a manner wholly different from the Eleusinian or Orphic mysteries; just as Dante and Aquinas are remote from the authors of the Gospels; yet in both cases the later figures emerge from a living and unbroken tradition. This is very different from personal interpretation and the borrowing of myths in the service of ideas outside the tradition altogether.

Personal interpretation belongs more to our own century than to the eighteenth, for whom the language of mythology had been purged of the irrational. Bacon's interpretations of the Greek mythology as illustrative of natural processes (as the story of Demeter and Persephone of the sowing and harvesting of corn) commended themselves to the Enlightenment. It was against such interpretations Taylor launched his attack:

> . . . the reader may perceive how infinitely superior the explanation which the Platonic philosophy affords of these fables is to the frigid and trifling interpretations of Bacon and other modern mythologists; who are able indeed to point out their correspondence to something in the natural or moral world, because such is the wonderful connection of things, that all things sympathise with all, but are at the same time ignorant that these fables were framed by men divinely wise . . .

Mythology was already before Taylor's publications beginning to re-assert its perennial imaginative fascination; such works as Percy's translation of Mallet's *Northern Antiquities,* and Gray's interest in these and also in the Welsh 'antiquities' was one aspect of this revival of interest. Sir William Jones in his *Proceedings of the Calcutta Society of Bengal* encouraged the study of Hindu mythology and cosmogony. But more typical men of their age were Taylor's arch-enemy in the field of Greek mythology, Bishop Warburton, author of *The Divine Legation of Moses,* and Jacob Bryant, author of that Golden Bough of the eighteenth century, *A New System of Mythology.* This three-volume work is packed with erudition and beautifully illustrated with engravings, (some of which are by Blake, made during his apprenticeship with Basire) but all Bryant's learning was amassed in the service of premises which are perhaps not much more ridiculous than many of the present time – that all pagan pantheons are comprised of the eight persons who survived the Deluge in Noah's Ark. Sir William Jones considered that Bryant had not proved his point; Taylor alone ventured to say that such an idea was pure nonsense. He was no less outspoken on . . .

> . . . the extreme ridiculousness of Dr Warburton's system, that the grand secret of the mysteries consisted in exposing the errors of Polytheism, and in teaching the doctrine of the unity, or the existence of one deity alone. . . . . But it is by no means wonderful that men who have not the smallest conception of the true nature of the gods; who have persuaded themselves that they were only dead men deified; and who measure the understandings of the ancients by their own, should be led to fabricate a system so improbable and absurd. (A *Dissertation on the Eleusinian and Bacchic Mysteries.* R. & H. p. 524.)

Taylor's impatience was that of an intelligent man master of his subject with the 'pedants' and 'verbal critics' who mistook their abilities, and supposed that a knowledge of Greek grammar was the same thing as a knowledge of Greek philosophy. It was also fully justified by the total absence, among the English clergy of the eighteenth century, of any vestige of understanding of symbols.

Coleridge gave the name of 'printer's devil personifications' to those persons created in such profusion by the eighteenth-century poets of the Enlightenment by the simple typographical device of giving a capital letter to Justice, Chaos, Fancy, Mischance, Contemplation, Commerce, culminating in Erasmus Darwin's total subjection of the qualitative language of myth to the quantitative mentality of commercial enterprise in such figures as 'unconquer'd Steam' 'orient Nitre' and 'adamantine Steel'. Locke himself might have approved such a triumph of Reason. The Romantic poets had to rebuild mythological discourse from the ruins to which it had been reduced.

We can imagine with what a sense of triumphant liberation the young Romantic poets must have read Taylor's *Dissertation on the Mysteries of Eleusis and Dionysus*. This remains the best essay known to me upon the symbolic significance of these myths as understood within the tradition to which they belong. Blake immediately upon reading it wrote his own version of the myth of the two Goddesses, *The Little Girl Lost* and *The Little Girl Found*, a re-telling of the story taken, in almost every detail, from Taylor. These poems are the first truly mythological poems of the Romantic revival; their guise is strange, like no other poetry which had hitherto been written; yet they are truly Neoplatonic poems, for they imply the total view of the nature of things held also by the Hellenic philosophers and implicit in the Mysteries of Eleusis themselves. Blake's poems are not a personal interpretation of a mythological story; they are personal only in the form in which he embodies the traditional theme. He tells of the descent of the soul – the 'little girl', the *Kore* – who like Persephone wanders away from her mother, and, invoking night, 'descends' into the 'cave' of generated existence. The second poem tells, like the Greater Mysteries of Eleusis, óf the Mother's search for her child; and ends, like these Mysteries themselves, with an epiphany of the sacred nature of the soul's 'descent' and marriage to the King of the Underworld.

Taylor quotes extensively, in his *Dissertation*, from a book he later translated – Sallust *On the Gods and the Universe*. Sallust may be taken as the orthodox interpreter of a tradition still living at the time at which he wrote; and it was his interpretation of mythological discourse which was to transform English poetry, from Blake and Coleridge to Shelley and Keats. According to Sallust,

Of fables some are theological, others physical, others animastic (or relating to the soul), others material, and lastly, others mixed from these.

As an example of the purely theological fable Sallust instances Saturn devouring his children:

> for it insinuates nothing more than the nature of an intellectual god; since every intellect returns to itself . . . but we speculate fables physically when we speak concerning the energies of the gods about the world; as when considering Saturn the same as time, and calling the parts of time the children of the universe, we assert that the children are devoured by their parent. But we employ fables in an animastic mode when we contemplate the energies of the soul . . . Lastly, fables are material, such as the Egyptians ignorantly employ, considering and calling corporeal natures divinities; such as Isis, earth, Osiris, humidity, Typhon, heat; or, again, denominating Saturn, water, Adonis, fruits, and Bacchus, wine. (*Taylor, Selected Writings*, pp. 383–4)

This 'ignorant' mode of using myth was precisely what the materialist philosophers and such poets as followed them, from Bacon to Erasmus Darwin, had triumphantly produced as the fruits of their enlightenment; 'but to call them gods', says Sallust, 'is alone the province of fools and mad men.' No one since the Renaissance had written of mythology as did Taylor; for symbol and myth is a discourse upon the qualitative nature of things; and by the end of the eighteenth century the modern fallacy was already well established, which confuses the quantitative and measurable aspect of things with their total 'reality'. Followers of the mechanistic philosophy feel no need of other terms in which to describe the universe.

Taylor proceeds to unfold the fable of Proserpine as 'properly of a mixed nature, or composed from all four species of fables, the theological, physical, animastic, and material'; and Blake follows him in every detail. It was from Taylor that Blake learned that imaginative yet precise use of the mythological language of which he is so great a master.

Taylor had already published in 1789 – two years before his

Dissertation on the Mysteries – a work twice reprinted during his lifetime: *The Mystical Hymns of Orpheus*; with a remarkable introductory essay on the Orphic theology, with its hierarchic series of dependent causes and triads of energies. Taylor's essay is the basis of G. R. S. Mead's book on Orphism, written at the time of the Theosophical revival of the Platonic tradition, at the end of the nineteenth century. These hymns have no literary merit in themselves; they were the hymnbook of some ancient temple where the cult of Dionysus was practised, but they are compact with what one may call the vocabulary, or alphabet of the symbolic attributes of the Greek pantheon; a symbolic language rich in suggestion and adequate to every purpose of exploring the qualitative aspects of the cosmos. As such the Orphic Hymns provided the Romantic poets with a dictionary from which to draw their symbolic themes. Taylor's exposition establishes these mythological symbols within the context of the metaphysical system of which they are properly a part. His translations and expositions of the Greek mythology brought about a revolution from which there was no possibility of return to the poetics of the Enlightenment, whose entrenched and complacent spokesmen are so castigated by Taylor himself. The victory was, as always, to the Sacred Majesty of Truth, whom he served.

With Coleridge and Shelley, who read Greek and Latin fluently, it is less easy than in the case of Blake to be sure that Taylor was the source of any particular theme, though the general influence of Taylor upon both poets is certain; both possessed at least some of his works. However, there are a few clear instances. There is a long note – almost an essay in itself – to Taylor's translation of Porphyry's *De Antro Nympharum* on the symbolism of the sea-voyage of Odysseus;

> For this whole story relates to the descent of the soul into this terrene body, and its wanderings and punishments, till it returns to its true country and pristine felicity.

Taylor goes through the sequence of Ulysses' adventures, 'through his various wanderings and woes, till he recovers the ruined empire of his soul.' There are many details which suggest that here Coleridge found the theme of his 'Rime of the Ancient Mariner'.

Shelley, like Coleridge, was a Greek scholar; he owned a copy of Taylor's Plato, and perhaps a careful search in the writings of both might bring to light details to prove that Shelley had not only possessed but read these volumes. Shelley's *Defence of Poetry* is a work even more generally and minutely Platonic than Coleridge's *Biographia;* and the revolution in the use of mythology was, in Shelley, complete: Platonic polytheism had become the language of English poetry, not in the purely decorative sense in which Pope and Dryden adorned country squires and their elegant daughters with the names of gods and nymphs, but as a language of qualitative and metaphysical discourse. The Hellenistic revolution Taylor had set in train finds in Shelley its most complete expression.

Daemons were to Shelley especially dear; Taylor had added as a note to his translation of the First Alcibiades (1804) Proclus On the Daimon of Socrates, but not until 1820 did his translation of Apuleius' *On the God of Socrates* – which appears to have been Shelley's chief source – appear; Shelley could not, therefore, have read Apuleius in Taylor's translation. But Taylor published in the *Classical Journal* (XVI, Sept. 1817) 'Remarks on the Daemon of Socrates', which Shelley might have seen. At most we can surmise that Taylor's profession of polytheism had in Shelley made a passionate proselyte, and sent him to the original works.

Apuleius appears to be the source of a beautiful and familiar chorus from *Prometheus Unbound*:

> From unremembered ages we
> Gentle guides and guardian be
> Of heaven-oppressed mortality;
> And we breathe, and sicken not,
> The atmosphere of human thought:
> Be it dim, and dank, and gray,
> Like a storm-extinguished day,
> Travelled o'er by dying gleams;
>   Be it bright as all between
> Cloudless skies and windless streams,
>   Silent, liquid, and serene;
> As the birds within the wind,
>   As the fish within the wave,
> As the thoughts of Man's own mind
>   Float through all above the grave;

> We make there our liquid lair,
> Voyaging cloudlike and unpent
> Through the boundless element . . .

No poetry could be more entirely removed from the Lockean or Behaviourist view of the passivity of the mind before 'nature'; here mind itself is the 'boundless element' through which living energies travel. Such discourse assumes something of the order Jung attempted to describe under the name of a 'collective unconscious' or transpersonal mind peopled by animate archetypal figures. All such terms are more or less inadequate, and the old names of 'gods' and 'daemons' (translated by the Christian Platonist Dionysius the Areopagite into the celestial hierarchies of angels) seem after all the best yet devised.

According to Apuleius the element of those Shelley-like beings is air. The daemons (I quote from Taylor's translation) . . .

> . . . are in their genus animals [that is to say, animate beings], in their species rational, in mind passive, in body aereal, and in time perpetual. As they are media between us and the Gods, in the place of their habitation, so likewise in the nature of their mind; having immortality in common with the Gods, and passion in common with other natures subordinate to themselves.

Yeats calls these passionate immortal energies, the 'moods' or 'gate-keepers':

> Time drops in decay
> Like a candle burnt out,
> And the mountain and woods
> Have their day, have their day;
> What one of the rout
> Of the fire-born moods
> Has fallen away?

Daemons are of the province of intermediate spirits between earth and heaven, the human and the supernal realm; for . . .

> the life there is eternal and never-failing, but is here decaying and interrupted; and the natures there are elevated to

beatitude, but these that are here are depressed to calamity. What then? Does nature connect itself by no bond?

The daemons are this bond and medium: 'They transmit prayers from the one, and gifts from the other.' They govern dreams, and the flight of birds.

> . . . if the clouds fly loftily, all of which originate from, and again flow downward to, the earth, what should you at length think of the bodies of daimons, which are much less dense, and therefore so much more attenuated than clouds? For they are not conglobed from a feculent nebula and a tumid darkness, as the clouds are, but they consist of that most pure, liquid and serene element of air, and on this account are not easily visible to the human eye, unless they exhibit an image of themselves by divine command . . . the frame of their bodies is rare, splendid, and attenuated, so that they pass through the rays of the whole of our sight by their rarity, reverberate them by their splendour, and escape them by their subtlety.

Shelley's chorus is obviously based upon this passage.

It is likely that Apuleius was himself using the names of the material elements – air, ether, earth – in a figurative sense, or at all events a qualitative sense; and in this Shelley much resembles him, whose cloud, wind, sky and ocean are spiritually animate in a way more precise than the word 'pantheism' implies; the life of Shelley's elements, whether of mind or of nature, is, in the Platonic sense of the word, daemonic.

I know of no direct evidence of Keats having read Taylor; very likely he had – Bernard Blackstone in his *The Consecrated Urn* gives this as his view. He was, (as Dr Ian Jack has shown in his *Keats and the Mirror of Art*) more influenced by the visual than by the philosophic aspect of the Greek myths. Yet his use of the figures of Saturn, Apollo, and Mnemosyne in the 'Hyperion' fragments are all strictly in accordance with the Orphic theology; the doctrine of knowledge by recollection (anamnesis) embodied in the figure of Moneta or Mnemosyne is that of Plato himself. By the time Keats came to write, Plato and the Orphic theology were in the air, and he adopts them rather as we do current usage than as a poet who is forging a new imaginative world, as Blake was.

Taylor himself was no poet; his verse renderings of the Orphic and other classical hymns have no literary merit. In his later years his friends do not seem to have been poets or artists; there is no evidence that his acquaintance with Flaxman was resumed after the sculptor's return from Italy. Some of Taylor's books passed into the Coleridge family after the death both of the poet and of Taylor himself, but there is no evidence that the two ever met. Taylor was a mathematician and a metaphysician; he could not have foreseen that his call to the standard of Plotinus would be answered in English only by the poets, and a few painters; he probably would have hoped for something more like what happened in America, where Emerson and Bronson Alcott and their circle of New England Transcendentalists studied and discussed his works as they dreamed of a new society, a new system of education, even a new religion, to be founded upon Platonic principles; and where a magazine, *The Platonist*, (1881–8) edited by Thomas M. Johnson, was devoted to the study and dissemination of Taylor's writings. (See *Thomas Taylor in America* by George Mills Harper, R. & H.)

With the exceptions of Berkeley (an Irishman) and a few others, the Platonic tradition in England has been kept alive by the poets. Yeats said that the English have the poorest philosophical literature of any European nation; we might reply that English poetry, in compensation, is the most profoundly philosophic poetry in Europe; and the philosophy of poetry – the language of imagination, as Shelley said – cannot be other than Platonism, or some kindred version of that philosophy which takes mind not matter as its first principle and ground. Materialist knowledge may produce technology but it can never produce art, since it denies the very foundations of imaginative thought, Coleridge's 'facts of mind'; and, with Locke and the Behaviourists, makes mind purely passive before nature.

As for Taylor himself, though Emerson rightly calls him a 'feeder of poets', his gifts were not literary; but G. R. S. Mead, in his preface to a reprint of one of his volumes of Plotinus, published in 1914, called him 'a wonderful genius and profound philosopher':

It is true that the perfected scholarship of our own times demands a higher standard of translation than Taylor presents; but what was true of his critics then is true of his critics today: though they may know more Greek, he knew more Plato. Taylor was more than a scholar, he was a philosopher in the Platonic sense of the word.

6 Blake, Wordsworth and Nature

In venturing to compare these two great contemporaries, Wordsworth and Blake, I shall have little new to say about Wordsworth; anything new I may have to say will be about Blake. Wordsworth's poetry, in any case, like Shakespeare, is part of us. To some – like myself, much of whose childhood was lived in Northumberland – Wordsworth's spacious and majestic record of his youth is like a memory of our own. To others less fortunate he has given a truer memory than falls to the lot of the children of suburb and industrial city. For we are all children of the one green and rocky earth; nature is an ancestral memory which must always seem more native to us, more familiar, than city streets.

To the Victorians Wordsworth was more than a poet, he was a religion, and the Lake District a national shrine. Now it is sacred texts from *The Marriage of Heaven and Hell* that a younger generation chalks on the walls of Blake's London, that 'Human awful wonder of God': (K. 665) for that generation is more concerned with humanity than with nature. But it was Blake who wrote:

> Great things are done when Men & Mountains meet,
> This is not done by Jostling in the Street.
>
> (K. 550)

There is no proof that those words, written in his notebook, referred to Wordsworth, though they may very well have done so. The two poets had after all so much in common. Both were in revolt against the diction and poetic theories of Dr Johnson and the Augustans; both aspired to write an epic poem to equal Milton; both were poets of childhood; both were influenced by Rousseau in their pleading the cause of 'free' love. Both Blake and Wordsworth had deeply realized that a man is more than his reason, and wrote from feeling and imagination. Both poets had been fortunate – Wordsworth because he was a country boy, Blake because he had been able to persuade his father to send him to an art-school – in eluding the education of the period which made a child (in Wordsworth's words) 'no Child, but a Dwarf Man', 'a monster birth' (*The Prelude* V. I. 295. Ed. de Selincourt, p. 150 hereafter *Works*) produced by intellectual and moral cramming.

But if there is much in common in their views of man, how different the human scene and setting presented by these two poets. Wordsworth saw human beings in a rural environment to which he felt that we rightly belong. He recalls how as a boy he would sometimes meet a shepherd on the fells, and he saw in such men the very type of human dignity:

> . . . on rainy days
> Mine eyes have glanced upon him, few steps off,
> In size a giant, stalking through the fog,
> His sheep like Greenland Bears; at other times
> When round some shady promontory turning
> His form hath flashed upon me, glorified
> By the deep radiance of the setting sun:
> Or him have I descried in distant sky,
> A solitary object and sublime
> Above all height!
> (*Prelude* [1805 version] VIII 1. 385–407)

Blake was the supreme poet of the industrial revolution; but that is not to say that he saw in it the dawn of his new age: on the contrary, he deplored and denounced the enslavement of 'the myriads of eternity' to the 'mills and ovens and cauldrons' made in the image of a mechanized nature: with sorrow he wrote of the Giant Albion, 'his machines are woven with his life'. The enslavement of men and women and children to industry he condemned not only or principally because of the low wages, the 'pittance' of the 'crust of bread' for which they must sell their humanity; above all the dehumanizing nature of the work itself filled him with wrath. He would have welcomed those who call for an end to our destructive use of the resources of the world and a return to 'the simple rules of life' by which the living earth sustains all her creatures. He was himself a craftsman – an engraver by profession – and loved the tools and skills of the workman that he saw everywhere being abandoned:

> . . . the plow & harrow, the loom,
> The hammer & the chisel & the rule & compasses. . . .
> (K. 699)

With the industrial revolution all that age-old simple skill is lost:

> . . . all the Arts of Life they chang'd into the Arts of Death in Albion.
> The hour-glass contemn'd because its simple workmanship
> Was like the workmanship of the plowman, & the water wheel
> That raises water into cisterns, broken & burn'd with fire
> Because its workmanship was like the workmanship of the shepherd;
> And in their stead, intricate wheels invented, wheel without wheel,
> To perplex youth in their outgoings & to bind to labours in Albion
> Of day & night the myriads of eternity: that they may grind
> And polish brass & iron hour after hour, laborious task,
> Kept ignorant of its use: that they might spend the days of wisdom
> In sorrowful drudgery to obtain a scanty pittance of bread.
> (K. 700)

For Blake too man's true world is a pastoral world, and the Schoolboy of his *Songs of Innocence* enjoys just those country pleasures Wordsworth knew. Blake's cities are the bitter world of Experience where Paradise is lost.

Wordsworth has no less to say about humanity than has Blake; and Blake, on his side, no less than Wordsworth to say about nature, though he cannot be called a 'nature poet', in the Wordsworthian sense. For Wordsworth re-creates nature for us as he himself experienced its presence. His grandeur lies in the spaciousness, the freedom, the majestic solitude and the all-embracing wholeness of his 'nature'. Like Constable he had turned from the eighteenth century prospect of nature 'improved' by art to the wilderness itself and 'the spirit of the place.' Like Constable Wordsworth gloried above all in the untamed elements:

> . . . The immeasurable height
> Of woods decaying, never to be decay'd
> The stationary blasts of water-falls,
> And every where along the hollow rent
> Winds thwarting winds, bewilder'd and forlorn,
> The torrents shooting from the clear blue sky,
> The rocks that mutter'd close upon our ears,
> Black drizzling crags that spake by the way-side

As if a voice were in them, the sick sight
And giddy prospect of the raving stream,
The unfetter'd clouds, and region of the Heavens,
Tumult and peace, the darkness and the light
Were all like workings of one mind, the features
Of the same face, blossoms upon one tree,
Characters of the great Apocalypse,
The types and symbols of Eternity,
Of first and last, and midst, and without end.
(*Prelude* VI. 1. 556–73)

When Wordsworth describes minute things, these are seen as parts in the one great whole,

Rolled round in Earth's diurnal course
With rocks and stones and trees
(*A Slumber did my Spirit Seal, Works* II, p. 216)

When he writes of:

A violet by a mossy stone
Half hidden from the eye,
Fair as a star, when only one
Is shining in the sky

flower and star are situated together in the firmament. Or from *Resolution and Independence* the lonely leach-gatherer, merged with nature's solitudes:

Upon the margin of that moorish flood
Motionless as a cloud the old Man stood
That heareth not the lone winds as they call
And moveth all together, if it move at all.
(*Resolution and Independence, Works* II, p. 237)

Wordsworth could say with truth of feeling,

To me the meanest flower that blows can give
Thoughts that do often lie too deep for tears.
(*Intimations of Immortality, Works* IV, p. 285)

Yet he is most himself 'when men and mountains meet,' waterfall and crag, wind, cloud, and those bare heights beyond the last sheepfold of the hills; and above all the play of all the elements that together make up the single mighty being of Earth.

With Blake it is otherwise;

> To see a World in a Grain of Sand,
> And a Heaven in a Wild Flower,
> Hold Infinity in the palm of your hand
> And Eternity in an hour.
>
> (K. 431)

It is in the heart of the minute that Blake found his 'types and symbols of Eternity'. Where Wordsworth stands in awe before the vast, so does Blake before the minute, where for him the mystery lies. He delights in the insect-world because these creatures so well express that mystery of the minute. The characters in the great Apocalypse are for Blake the vermin of the 'wine-press' of the great vintage of the earth:

> . . . the little Seed,
> The sportive Root, the Earth-worm, the gold Beetle, the wise Emmet
> Dance round the Wine-presses of Luvah: the Centipede is there,
> The ground Spider with many eyes, the Mole clothed in velvet,
> The ambitious Spider in his sullen web, the lucky golden Spinner,
> The Earwig arm'd, the tender Maggot, emblem of immortality,
> The Flea, Louse, Bug, the Tape-Worm, all the Armies of Disease
> Visible or invisible to the slothful vegetating Man.
> The slow Slug, the grasshopper that sings & laughs & drinks:
> Winter comes, he folds his slender bones without a murmur.
> The cruel Scorpion is there, the Gnat, Wasp, Hornet & the Honey
> Bee,
> The Toad & venomous Newt, the Serpent cloth'd in gems & gold.
> They throw off their gorgeous raiment: they rejoice with loud jubilee
>
> (K. 513)

Blake's creatures are not – like Virgil's vermin of the threshing-floor which no doubt suggested Blake's – realistic. They belong to the world of bestiary and fable. But it is to Swedenborg that this catalogue of creatures points – Swedenborg, whose *Angelic Wisdom concerning the Divine Love and the Divine Wisdom* Blake lovingly annotated at the very outset of his poetic life, in about 1788. In that work there are many passages which seem to have inspired Blake's insect Bacchanalia. Swedenborg was by profession a scientist (he was Assessor of Minerals to the Swedish Government) – and had the eye of a naturalist. Compare Blake's 'armies of disease' with Swedenborg's

> . . . noxious insects fill the atmosphere in clouds, and noxious vermin walk the earth in armies, and consume herbs to the very roots. I once observed in my garden, in the space of an ell that almost all the dust was turned into very small insects, which on being stirred with a stick rose in clouds.

Swedenborg had also a naturalist's habit of cataloguing, as in this (one among several) list of animals classified according to their 'evil uses', as he says:

> . . . we have poisonous serpents, scorpions, crocodiles, great snakes, horned owls, screech owls, mice, locusts, frogs, spiders; also flies, drones, moths, lice, mites, in a word, creatures that consume grasses, leaves, fruits, seeds, meat and drink; and that do hurt beasts and man; in the vegetable kingdom we have malignant, virulent and poisonous herbs, and leguminous plants and shrubs . . . (*Divine Love and Wisdom*, 338)

So in Blake also we have 'the Nettle that stings with soft down;' and 'The indignant Thistle'.

Swedenborg draws a clear line of distinction between good and evil creatures; his good animals are of the duller kind, 'elephants, camels, horses, mules, oxen, sheep, goats and others which are of the herd or the flock'. (op. cit. para. 346) But Blake, in his belief that 'everything that lives is holy' (K. 289 and 192), presents his insect swarms in the eternal delight of their energy; and indeed Swedenborg too saw the marvel of the minute lives of his garden pests:

> Each one of these insects is organized to feel and to move, and is furnished therefore with fibres and vessels, and with little hearts, pulmonary pipes, minute viscera, and brains. (op. cit. para. 352)

Blake must have been delighted with this and similar passages; for in *Milton* he recalls it:

Seest thou the little winged fly, smaller than a grain of sand?
It has a heart like thee, a brain open to heaven & hell,
Withinside wondrous & expansive,: its gates are not clos'd:
I hope thine are not: hence it clothes itself in rich array:
Hence thou art cloth'd with human beauty, O thou mortal man.
Seek not thy heavenly father then beyond the skies,
There Chaos dwells & ancient Night & Og & Anak old.

(K. 502)

Og and Anak are scriptural types of giants, and Blake situates them, appropriately, in those Newtonian vast spaces whose emptiness he contrasts with the infinity and eternity of life in the smallest of creatures. The least of things, flowers, worm and fly, grain of sand and particle of dust are Blake's chosen symbols of 'the infinite in all things'. There is nothing in Blake's vision of the minute of that sentimental false humility which delights in self-denigration. The dignity of every creature is not relative but absolute. In those familiar lines quoted earlier, look at the implied equations: a grain of sand is a whole world, and the petals of a wild flower are all heaven; and yet on this grain of sand, the earth, we may know infinity, and in the ephemeral hour of life experience eternity.

In a passage in *Jerusalem* Blake uses the same images, but reversing their force: that mighty earth with its record of great civilisations which to reason seems so imposing in scale and grandeur is but a grain of sand, and the heavens of the astronomer's night sky, a moth's wing:

. . . all his pyramids were grains
Of sand, & his pillars dust on the fly's wing, & his starry
Heavens a moth of gold & silver, mocking his anxious grasp.
Thus Los alter'd his Spectre, & every Ratio of his Reason
He alter'd time after time . . .

(K. 739)

Without wishing to minimise Blake's genius, it must be said that the ideas to which he gave vesture so original are seldom his own. Apart from the major influence of Swedenborg, Blake drew upon many sources within 'the one unanimous and universal tradition'. From the German mystic Jakob Boehme, for example, (whom Blake supremely admired) come those images of 'the opening of the centres of the birth of life' which lend such spiritual depth to his images of the minute. According to Boehme every life is an original creation entering 'nature' from eternity through that dimensionless

> Point, Locus or place (where the Holy Ghost in the Birth of the Heart of God, in Paradise, did open infinite and innumerable Centres) in the eternal Birth. (*Three Principles of the Divine Essence*, Ch. IV, para. 72, Works I, p. 32)

Boehme writes

> The Eternal Center, and the Birth of Life, are everywhere. If you make a small Circle, as small as a little Grain (or Kernel of Seed) there is the whole Birth of the Eternal Nature. (*Mysterium Magnum* Ch. 43, para. 9 Works III, p. 253)

Blake uses Boehme's terminology in many passages; and restates the older mystic's gloss on the Gospel teaching that the Kingdom of Heaven is like a grain of mustard seed:

> The Vegetative Universe opens like a flower from the Earth's center
> In which is Eternity. It expands in Stars to the Mundane Shell
> And there it meets Eternity again, both within and without
>
> (K. 633)

Great things and small alike exist in the eternity of Imagination so Blake chooses the smallest sweetest flowers as most apt illustrations of the dimensionless *points* of the centres of the birth of life. In a passage of rare beauty he describes 'the break of day', with the opening of that day's flowers, not as a symbol of creation but as creation itself everywhere and always enacted:

> Thou perceivest the Flowers put forth their precious Odours,
> And none can tell how from so small a center come such sweets,
> Forgetting that within that Center Eternity expands

Its ever during doors that Og & Anak fiercely guard.
First, e'er the morning breaks, joy opens in the flowery bosoms,
Joy even to tears, which the Sun rising dries; first the Wild Thyme
And Meadow-sweet, downy & soft waving among the reeds,
Light springing on the air, lead the sweet Dance: they wake
The Honeysuckle sleeping on the Oak; the flaunting beauty
Revels along upon the wind; the White-thorn, lovely May,
Opens her many lovely eyes listening; . . .

(K. 520)

The centre is a door, a heart of joy, an opened eye; and so too the heart of every bird is a centre of eternity. Such is Blake's lark,

His little throat labours with inspiration; every feather
On throat & breast & wings vibrates with the effluence Divine.
All Nature listens silent to him, & the awful Sun
Stands still upon the Mountain looking on this little Bird
With eyes of soft humility & wonder, love & awe.

(K. 520)

It is not the bird who looks at the sun; the sun looks at the bird in 'awe'; for the 'effluence divine' comes not from space or size, but from the infinite within.

It would be unjust to Blake to say that 'nature' is for him no more than a philosophical idea. The meadow-sweet 'downy & soft waving among the reeds/Light springing on the air', or the May that 'Opens her many lovely eyes', or the

. . . little monsters
Who sit mocking upon the little pebbles of the tide . . .

(K. 296)

are beautifully observed, or the line Yeats admired,

Like the gay fishes on the wave, when the cold moon drinks the dew.
(K. 243)

But Blake often lacks what Wordsworth never fails to bring to his poetry, the existential encounter. The sparrow's nest Wordsworth and his sister found as children inspired a sense of delight and awe which owes nothing to philosophy:

Behold, within the leafy shade
Those bright blue eggs together laid!
On me the chance-discovered sight
Gleamed like a vision of delight.
I started — seeming to espy
The home and sheltered bed,
The Sparrow's dwelling, which hard by
My Father's house, in wet or dry
My sister Emmeline and I
Together visited.
(*The Sparrow's Nest. Works* I. p. 227)

To the poet it is 'a vision of delight'; to his sister a mystery almost too sacred to approach:

She looked at it and seemed to fear it;
Dreading, tho' wishing, to be near it.

Wordsworth does not define or analyse the instinctive emotion of the children at the sight of the birds' eggs in the nest; and yet is not the sense of the holy a recognition of the mystery of 'the centers of the birth of life'? Blake's spiritual knowledge and Wordsworth's truth of feeling are at one.

At the risk of shocking those lovers of Blake who see in him a visionary of absolute originality, I must say that with better knowledge of Blake's own deep studies it seems to me that his most remarkable gift was that of imaginatively assimilating the ideas of his chosen teachers. There is that beautiful verse-letter to his friend Thomas Butts in which Blake is reflecting on Newton's materialist theory of the structure of light:

The Atoms of Democritus
And Newton's Particles of light . . .
(K. 418)

of which he elsewhere wrote. These particles are Blake's starting-point:

The Light of the Morning
Heaven's Mountains adorning:
In particles bright
The jewels of Light
Distinct shone & clear.

(The 'distinct particles' come from Newton)

> Amaz'd & in fear
> I each particle gazed,
> Astonish'd, Amazed;
> For each was a Man
> Human-form'd. Swift I ran,
> For they beckon'd to me
> Remote by the Sea,
> Saying: Each grain of Sand,
> Every Stone on the Land,
> Each rock & each hill,
> Each fountain & rill,
> Each herb & each tree,
> Mountain, hill, earth & sea,
> Cloud, Meteor & Star,
> Are Men Seen Afar.
>
> (K. 804)

With due respect to Blake the 'vision' of nature he so unforget-
tably describes is not his own (except by adoption) but again
Swedenborg's. This passage is a superbly imagined realization of
Swedenborg's teaching that 'Heaven as a whole, and in every
part, is in form as a man', and the form of heaven 'in its greatest
and least things is like itself' . . . 'God is a man, and the created
universe is His image,' (*Divine Love and Wisdom*, para. 11)
Swedenborg again and again insists and Blake in his verse-letter
is gloriously dismissing Newton's theory of light as material
particles. No, says Blake, secure in the authority of his master,
'each was a Man, Human-form'd'; and so with 'Each grain of
Sand/Every Stone on the Land.'

Swedenborg, comparing the whole creative evolution of the
universe to the life-cycle of a plant which begins and ends in a
seed, writes of trees

Their primes are seeds, their ultimates are stems, clothed
with bark, and through the inner bark which is the ultimate
of their stems, they tend to seeds which, as was said, are
their primes. The stems clothed with layers of bark represent
the globe clothed with earths [Swedenborg means minerals]
from which the creation and formation of all uses exist. That

vegetations are brought about through the outer and inner barks and coatings by pushes through the envelopes of the roots continued around the stalks and branches into the initiaments of the fruits, and likewise through the fruits into the seeds, is known to many . . . It is plain that the progression of the creation of the universe was from its Prime, namely the Lord encircled by the sun, to ultimates, which are earths, and from these through uses to its Prime or Lord. (*Divine Love and Wisdom*, para. 314)

Here (from the early Prophetic poem *Vala*) is Blake's gloss, with help from Spenser and Milton, on Swedenborg:

> . . . the rough rocks groaning vegetate.
> . . . .
> The barked Oak, the long-limb'd Beech, the Chestnut tree, the Pine,
> The Pear tree mild, the frowning Walnut, the sharp Crab, & Apple
> sweet,
> The rough bark opens; twittering peep forth little beaks & wings,
> The Nightingale, the Goldfinch, Robin, Lark, Linnet & Thrush.
> The Goat leap'd from the craggy cliff, the Sheep awoke from the
> mould,
> Upon its green stalk rose the Corn, waving innumerable.

> (K. 269)

The 'groaning' rocks allude to St Paul's words (Romans 8. 22) 'the whole creation groaneth and travaileth in pain together' to bring forth the fruits of the spirit.

Swedenborg did not originate the idea of a cosmic God-man scattered or 'distributed' throughout nature and to be reassembled through the evolutionary struggle of creation. This process was the 'great work' of the Alchemists; and goes back (to take it no farther) to the myth of Osiris, whose dismembered body, scattered over the earth, was gathered and reassembled by Isis. And in one of his most eloquent early passages Blake writes of the regeneration of 'the eternal man':

> And as the seed waits Eagerly watching for it flower & fruit,
> Anxious its little soul looks out into the clear expanse
> To see if hungry winds are abroad with their invisible army,
> So Man looks out in tree & herb & fish & bird & beast

Collecting up the scatter'd portions of his immortal body
Into the Elemental forms of every thing that grows.
He tries the sullen north wind, riding on its angry furrows,
The sultry south when the sun rises, & the angry east
When the sun sets; when the clods harden & the cattle stand
Drooping & the birds hide in their silent nests, he stores his thoughts
As in a store house in his memory; he regulates the forms
Of all beneath & all above, & in the gentle West
Reposes where the Sun's heat dwells; he rises to the Sun
And to the Planets of the Night, & to the stars that gild
The Zodiac, & the stars that sullen stand to north & south.
He touches the remotest pole, & in the center weeps
That Măn should Labour & sorrow, & learn & forget, & return
To the dark valley whence he came, to begin his labour anew.
In pain he sighs, in pain he labours in his universe,
Screaming in birds over the deep, & howling in the wolf
Over the Slain, & moaning in the cattle, & in the winds,
And weeping over Orc & Urizen in clouds & flaming fires,
And in the cries of birth & in the groans of death his voice
Is heard throughout the Universe: wherever a grass grows
Or a leaf buds, The Eternal Man is seen, is heard, is felt,
And all his sorrows, till he reassumes his ancient bliss.

(K. 355–6)

Not figuratively but actually all creatures are 'men seen afar'
because the whole universe is the mystical body of 'the Divine
Humanity'.

Wordsworth too felt the presence of

> A motion and a spirit, that impels
> All thinking things, all objects of all thought,
> And rolls through all things.
> (*Lines written a few miles above* Tintern Abbey, *Works*
> II p. 262)

But for Wordsworth the natural elements are not 'men seen afar';
on the contrary, it was the non-human that overwhelmed the boy
who in a stolen boat rowed out in the evening on Ullswater:

> . . . . lustily
> I dipp'd my oars into the silent Lake,
> And, as I rose upon the stroke, my Boat

Went heaving through the water, like a Swan;
When from behind that craggy Steep, till then
The bound of the horizon, a huge Cliff,
As if with voluntary power instinct,
Uprear'd its head. I struck, and struck again,
And, growing still in stature, the huge Cliff
Rose up between me and the stars, and still,
With measur'd motion, like a living thing,
Strode after me. With trembling hands I turn'd,
And through the silent water stole my way
Back to the Cavern of the Willow tree.
There, in her mooring-place, I left my Bark,
And, through the meadows homeward went, with grave
And serious thoughts; and after I had seen
That spectacle, for many days, my brain
Work'd with a dim and undetermin'd sense
Of unknown modes of being; in my thoughts
There was a darkness, call it solitude,
Or Blank desertion, no familiar shapes
Of hourly objects, images of trees,
Of sea or sky, no colours of green fields;
But huge and mighty Forms that do not live
Like living men mov'd slowly through the mind
By day and were the trouble of my dreams.
(*The Prelude*, Book I, *Works* p. 22–4.)

What frightened Wordsworth in this experience was the failure of
what was for him (what is for all her creatures) a habitual trust
in that all-embracing presence of which he constantly speaks as
Nature in her feminine and maternal character. She is the sweet
familiar aspect of hills and streams, woods and fields and sky.
In Protestant England a too masculine, too moralistic, too rational
deity had left man without that 'refuge of sinners' the Catholic
world finds in the Blessed Virgin Mary; and through Wordsworth
a whole nation too long deprived of the archetype of the feminine,
compassionate, protective embrace of the Great Mother found
shelter and respite in Wordsworth's Nature, that

> . . . never did betray
> The heart that loved her.

'The Pope supposes Nature & the Virgin Mary to be the same
allegorical personages', Blake wrote. Whatever the Pope may

have supposed, 'Nature' for Protestant England was to become, through Wordsworth, the same all-merciful protectress to whom Catholic sinners turn 'now and in the hour of our death.'

Blake did not identify Nature with the Holy Virgin whom he calls Jerusalem, 'mother of souls'. Vala, or 'The Goddess Nature', is for Blake the mother of bodies, the cruel female will of the single indivisible process of generation and death. Yet we instinctively respond to the truth Wordsworth tells; a truth felt by the senses, known to every child who has been free to come and go, as Wordsworth was, within a countryside experienced as a portion of his very life,

> . . . a passion, She!
> A rapture often, and immediate joy
> (*The Prelude* Book VIII, 485–7)

Was it Aldous Huxley who somewhere said how differently inhabitants of more desert regions of the earth – in the earth-quake zone, perhaps – would respond to Wordsworth's comforting doctrine? Yet he instinctively perceived a truth Darwin was later to formulate as the principle of 'adaptation to environment'. Every creature on earth has its nest, its place within the whole. The skylark has its 'nest upon the dewy ground',

> Thy nest which thou canst drop into at will
> (*Works* II, 266)

– as the country people of Patterdale live in the sheltering embrace of their fells:

> . . . Immense
> Is the Recess, the circumambient World
> Magnificent, by which they are embraced.
> They move upon the soft green field:
> How little They, they and their doings seem,
> Their herds and flocks about them, they themselves,
> And all that they can further or obstruct!
> Through utter weakness pitiably dear
> As tender Infants are:

(how naturally Wordsworth chooses the image of the mother and child)

> . . . and yet how great!
> For all things serve them; them the Morning light
> Loves as it glistens on the silent rocks,
> And them the silent Rocks, which now from high
> Look down upon them; the reposing Clouds,
> The lurking Brooks from their invisible haunts,
> And Old Helvellyn, conscious of the stir,
> And the blue Sky that roofs their calm abode.
> (*The Prelude*, VIII 46–61. *Works* 286)

A century that had lost faith in God found its comfort in nature; but where, in our century that has driven human beings from their natural refuge, and has already wrought such destruction upon nature itself, are we to turn for that lost sense of security?

Only a year before his death, in 1826, Blake was reading Wordsworth's poems (the 1815 edition) and in the margin he wrote his objections to Wordsworth's view of nature.

> I see in Wordsworth the Natural Man rising up against the Spiritual Man Continually & then he is No Poet but a Heathen Philosopher at Enmity against all true poetry or Inspiration. (K. 782)

and beside these lines so dear to the Deist Victorians,

> And I could wish my days to be
> Bound each to each by natural piety,

> There is no such Thing as Natural Piety Because the Natural Man is at Enmity with God.

Wordsworth had, like Dante,

> Made This World the Foundation of All, & the Goddess Nature Memory is his Inspirer & not Imagination the Holy Ghost. (K. 785)

Blake could not agree with Wordsworth that the human mind is 'fitted' to nature; and called in question a passage in The Excursion,

> How exquisitely the individual Mind
> (And the progressive powers perhaps no less
> Of the whole species) to the external world
> Is fitted: – & how exquisitely too,
> Though this but little heard of among Men,
> The external world is fitted to the Mind.
>
> (*Works* V p. 5)

Blake saw suffering and evil as inherent in the mortal condition as such; only by shutting his eyes to other aspects of nature could Wordsworth show his goddess as kind. To Blake cruelty is in her very nature; he denounces the natural world as a torture-chamber, a lazar-house, prison and grave of the soul.

> Will you erect a lasting habitation in the mouldering Church yard?
> Or pillar & palace of Eternity in the jaws of the hungry grave?

For the materialist mortality must always be the nihil at the end of all:

> And the grave mock & laugh at the plow'd field, saying
> I am the nourisher, thou the destroyer; in my bosom is milk & wine,
> And a fountain from my breasts; to me come all multitudes;
> To my breath they obey; they worship me. I am a goddess & queen.
>
> (K. 354)

'Nature' is not only the smiling bride but the hag death. He quotes Wordsworth against himself:

> Such grateful haunts foregoing, if I oft
> Must turn elsewhere – to travel near the tribes
> And fellowships of Men, & see ill sights
> Of madding passions mutually inflamed,
> Must hear *Humanity in fields & groves*
> *Pipe solitary anguish*

(these words Blake underlined)

> Brooding above the fierce confederate storm
> Of Sorrow, barricaded evermore
> With the walls of cities . . .
>
> (*Works* V. 5)

Blake reminds Wordsworth in this marginal dialogue (for the two never met) that sorrow is not unknown even in 'fields and groves'.

> Does not this Fit, & is it not Fitting most Exquisitely too, but to what? – Not to Mind, but to the vile Body only & to its laws of Good & Evil & its Enmities against Mind.
>
> (K. 784)

Blake wrote, 'Wordsworth must know that what he writes valuable is not to be found in Nature,' and referred to Wordsworth's translation of Michelangelo's sonnet that contains the line

> Heaven-born, the Soul a heaven-ward course must hold.

Blake saw that there is no comfort in the natural world unless there is also knowledge of another.

For the natural philosophers nature is the substance, the soul a shadow; for Blake – in common with the entire tradition upon which he drew – it is nature that is the shadow; and his name for the Goddess Nature is 'the shadowy female'. Natural existence is only a shadow or reflection of eternity; and Swedenborg, using an ancient symbol, wrote that the image of God is in the created universe

> as a man's image is in a mirror, in which indeed the man appears, but still there is nothing of the man in it. (*Divine Love and Wisdom* para. 59)

Blake calls natural space 'the looking-glass of Enitharmon'. Plotinus used in this sense the myth of Narcissus, the boy who fell in love with his own reflection in the water; and there is in the *Hermetica* a more elaborate version of the myth in which the eternal man, falling in love with his own watery image, becomes merged in it, so that the image is animated with an unnatural life.

Blake himself made various attempts to tell this story; whose final realisation is the figure of Vala, the animated 'veil' of natural appearances; a shadow which develops 'a will of its own, perverse and wayward'. Vala is in reality only the reflected image of Jerusalem, the soul:

Vala is but thy Shadow, O thou lovliest among women!
A shadow animated by thy tears, O mournful Jerusalem!
Why wilt thou give to her a Body whose life is but a Shade?
Her Joy and love, a shade, a shade of sweet repose:
But animated and vegetated she is a devouring worm.

(K. 631)

In Vala's world 'Accident is formed Into Substance & Principle'
a reversal of the due order of things, for 'every Natural Effect
has a Spiritual Cause & Not/A Natural; for a Natural Cause
only seems'. (K. 513).

As usual Blake when he theorises about nature is paraphrasing
Swedenborg:

> . . . all things which exist in the natural world are effects
> and all things which exist in the Spiritual world are causes
> of these effects. The Natural, which does not derive its cause
> from the Spiritual, does not exist. (*Divine Love and Wisdom*,
> p. 134)

Vala 'The Goddess Nature' Blake saw as the seducer of the
Giant Albion, the English nation under the domination of the
materialist philosophy. The opaque 'veil', of the goddess Nature
was, as Blake says, 'formed into Substance and Principle' by
England's schools and universities totally committed to the
materialist view of the world.

The natural world only exists, according to Swedenborg (and
Blake follows him), by 'influx' from the spiritual world.

> The natural world is in itself inanimate and dead; the sun
> of the natural world is dead, and nature, because it derives
> origin from that sun is dead . . . the sun of the natural
> world is wholly dead, but the sun of the spiritual world is
> alive. (*Divine Love and Wisdom*, p. 157)

But even though 'the one sun is living and the other sun is dead
. . . the dead sun is itself created through the living sun'. Blake
in his writings had much to say of these two suns. The 'black'
sun of Nature is created in 'the dark void' when with the fall of
Urizen (natural reason) the world of generation is 'rent from

eternity'. This 'immense orb of fire', 'a Human Illusion/In Darkness and deep clouds involv'd' is 'black' because it gives no spiritual light;

> When Luvah's bulls each morning drag the sulphur Sun out of the
> Deep
> Harness'd with starry harness, black & shining, kept by black slaves
> (K. 503)

The slaves are 'black' for the same reason and in the same sense as the sun, to whose service their spiritual darkness condemns them.

It is to this 'black' sun that Blake uttered his defiance in another verse epistle to Thomas Butts. Los, the time-spirit, appears in the aspect of the natural sun:

> Then Los appear'd in all his power:
> In the Sun he appear'd, descending before
> My face in fierce flames; in my double sight
> 'Twas outward a Sun; inward Los in his might.

Blake defies this vision of the natural sun:

> This Earth breeds not our happiness.
> Another Sun feeds our life's streams,
> We are not warmed with thy beams;
> Thou measurest not the time to me,
> Nor yet the Space that I do see;
> My Mind is not with thy light array'd.
> Thy terrors shall not make me afraid.
> (K. 818)

– the terrors of natural time and space of which Los, as time-spirit, is the agent. This, again, is Swedenborg mythologized; but Swedenborg could never have written with the eloquence of Blake's magnificent reply to the positivists of his day:

> I assert for My Self that I do not behold the outward Creation & that to me it is hindrance & not Action; it is as the Dirt upon my feet, No part of Me. 'What', it will be Question'd, 'when the Sun rises, do you not see a round

disk of fire somewhat like a Guinea? 'O no, no, I see an
Innumerable company of the Heavenly host, crying 'Holy,
Holy, Holy is the Lord God Almighty.' I question not my
Corporeal or Vegetative Eye any more than I would Question
a Window concerning a Sight. I look thro' it & not with it.
(K. 617)

Which sun was it that Wordsworth loved? In the first version
of *The Prelude* he wrote:

> . . . a boy I loved the sun,
> Not as I since have loved him, as a pledge
> And surety of our earthly life, a light
> Which we behold and feel we are alive;
> Nor for his bounty to so many worlds
> But for this cause, that I had seen him lay
> His beauty on the morning hills, had seen
> The western mountain touch his setting orb,
> In many a thoughtless hour, when, from excess
> Of happiness, my blood appeared to flow
> For its own pleasure, and I breathed with joy.

– and so with the moon:

> Analogous the moon to me was dear;
> For I could dream away my purposes,
> Standing to gaze upon her while she hung
> Midway between the hills, as if she knew
> No other region; but belong'd to thee,
> Yea, appertain'd by a peculiar right
> To thee and thy grey huts, my darling Vale!
> (*The Prelude* II, 184–202. *Works* pp. 50–2).

Was it when Wordsworth began to love the sun for theoretical
reasons as 'a pledge and surety of our earthly life' that the
visionary gleam faded? If, as Swedenborg taught and Blake
believed, the light of the spiritual sun is wisdom, and its heat,
love, it seems that Wordsworth's sun darkened and cooled with
advancing years.

In the 1850 version of *The Prelude* he changed 'my darling
vale' – the cry of love – to 'thou (no longer 'my') one (no longer

'darling') dear Vale.' The line about the sun's 'bounty to so many worlds' is a Newtonian generalization; Wordsworth the man had begun to lose the boy's sense of its glory in his own. Blake would have deplored the changes made by Wordsworth the 'heathen philosopher' upon the vision of Wordsworth the boy. But how close is Wordsworth's first spontaneous response to Blake's own description of the sun of vision:

> The Sky is an immortal Tent built by the Sons of Los:
> And every Space that a Man views around his dwelling-place
> Standing on his own roof or in his garden on a mount
> Of twenty-five cubits in height, such space is his Universe:
> And on its verge the Sun rises & sets, the Clouds bow
> To meet the flat Earth & the Sea in such an order'd Space:
> The Starry heavens reach no further, but here bend and set
> On all sides, & the two Poles turn on their valves of gold;
> And if he move his dwelling-place, his heavens also move
> Where'er he goes, & all his neighbourhood bewail his loss.
>
> (K. 516)

If Wordsworth was within the orthodoxy of the natural philosophers Blake was within another, and older, orthodoxy when he wrote that he looked through not with his 'corporeal and vegetative eye'. Swedenborg is an immediate source, who challenged those who 'think from the eye and cannot think from the understanding'; (*Divine Love & Wisdom*, para. 46) and Plato himself uses the same figure: 'it is more proper to consider the eyes and ears as things through which than things by which, we perceive'. (Theatetus 184)

> If Perceptive Organs vary, Objects of Perception seem to vary:
> If the Perceptive Organs close, their Objects seem to close also.
>
> (K. 661)

To this view of the senses Blake was again and again to return. So, in *Europe*, 'Five windows light the cavern'd Man:' through which he can see 'small portions of the eternal world that ever groweth;' (K. 237) In *Visions of the Daughters of Albion*, Blake's most concentrated attack on Locke's view of the senses, Oothoon, the soul who remembers eternity laments, in the 'cave' of this world,

They told me that I had five senses to inclose me up,
And they inclos'd my infinite brain into a narrow circle,
And sunk my heart into the Abyss, a red, round globe, hot burning,
Till all from life I was obliterated and erased.

(K. 191)

In a passage three times repeated in different contexts Blake
describes the 'binding of Urizen', the 'eternal mind' into mortal
perception. The seven days of Creation are described, each day
as a woeful limitation imposed, until the terrible incarceration is
complete.

How, then, would the world appear to what Blake calls the
enlarged and infinite senses of 'the true Man'? (K. 98) There is
in *The Marriage of Heaven and Hell* an episode which tells how

> . . . on the abyss of the five senses, where a flat sided steep
> frowns over the present world, I saw a mighty Devil folded
> in black clouds, hovering on the sides of the rock: with
> corroding fires he wrote the following sentences now per-
> ceived by the minds of men, & read by them on earth:

> How do you know but ev'ry Bird that cuts the airy way,
> Is an immense world of delight, clos'd by your senses five?
> (K. 150)

Closed; for the senses exclude more of reality than they admit.

The cogency of Blake's argument is more evident now than
in the nineteenth century; as it has always been to the Indian
philosophies, and as it was to Berkeley, whose *Siris* Blake
annotated. Berkeley said of the things perceptible to us, 'their
esse is *percipi*' – things exist in being perceived. And Blake, 'I
know that this World is a World of Imagination & Vision'; 'To
Me This World is all One continued Vision of Fancy or Imagination.' (K. 793)

Yet Blake knew that 'Eternity is in love with the productions
of Time'; who, in the person of Los, measures out to human
kind each day's portion of the visions of eternity:

Thou seest the Constellations in the deep & wondrous Night:
They rise in order and continue their immortal courses
Upon the mountain & in vales with harp & heavenly song,

With flute & clarion, with cups & measures fill'd with foaming wine.
Glitt'ring the streams reflect the Vision of beatitude,
And the calm Ocean joys beneath & smooths his awful waves:
These are the Sons of Los, & these the Labourers of the Vintage.
Thou seest the gorgeous clothed Flies that dance & sport in summer
Upon the sunny brooks & meadows: every one the dance
Knows in its intricate mazes of delight artful to weave:
Each one to sound his instruments of music in the dance,
To touch each other & recede, to cross & change & return:
These are the Children of Los; thou seest the Trees on mountains,
The wind blows heavy, loud they thunder thro' the darksom sky,
Uttering prophecies & speaking instructive words to the sons
Of men: These are the Sons of Los: These the Visions of Eternity,
But we see only as it were the hem of their garments
When with our vegetable eyes we view these wondrous Visions.

(K. 511–12)

In such passages as this Blake rises to a sublime vision of
nature Wordsworth himself has never surpassed.

7 Innocence and Experience

Before we look more closely at Blake's *Songs of Innocence and Experience* it would be well to ask why he wrote them. Already in the answers to this question we shall discover that, as in all Blake's writings, wherever we find apparent simplicity there are deeper issues involved than we had thought. Historically the answer could be simple enough; during the late eighteenth century poems were for the first time being written for children by those concerned with education. The hymn-writer Isaac Watts, for example, had published *Divine Songs for Children*, and *Moral Songs*, whose 'language and Measures should be easy and flowing with Cheerfulness, and without the Solemnities of Religion . . . that the Children might find Delight and Profit together.' These poems remained popular for a century and more; my father knew most or many of them by heart (having been taught them in school) and indeed I learned some of them myself as a child. To Watts we shall return, for Blake had evidently read his Songs with attention, and much indignation.

But Watts himself – and there were others – were themselves products of their time. Childhood was for the first time being considered by philosophers in relation to theories of knowledge; and this in its turn produced a prolific crop of theories of education.

Locke had much to say on the nature of knowledge. His view was that all knowledge comes to us through the senses. A newborn child is like a blank page on which nothing has yet been written, and on which anything can be written that the educators choose; there was much talk among followers of Locke about the 'forming' of the infant mind – a process of conditioning that could not begin too soon. According to Locke there are no innate ideas:

If we will attentively consider new-born *Children* we shall
have little Reason, to think that they bring many Ideas into
the World With them. For, bating, perhaps, some faint
Idea's, of Hunger, and Thirst, and Warmth, and some
Pains, which they may *have* felt in the Womb, there is *not*
the least appearance of any settled Idea's at all in them . . .
One may perceive how, that they get no more, nor no
other, than what Experience and the Observation of things,
that come in their way, furnish them with; which might be
enough to satisfie us, that they are not Original Characters,
stamped on the Mind.

This is a view much like modern Behaviourism, which sees life
as a matter of reflexes conditioned in beings themselves to be
regarded as mechanisms. The brain is considered as if it were the
mind which controls it, and described as a highly receptive computer 'programmed' by education. This evil view is false because
it considers man in merely quantitative terms and denies all levels
of being except the physical. Indeed Blake from the beginning to
the end of his writing life strove to answer and expose the fallaci-
ous teaching of Locke, regarding Locke's materialism as a view
of humanity as destructive as it is false. He had already given
much thought to Locke before he wrote *Songs of Innocence*, his
radiantly inspired answer to a false philosophy prevalent in his
day, and still clung to by a majority in our own: the materialist
view of man and his mental processes accepted as axiomatic by
the framers of programmes for the mass media, and, if questioned
by some of the best scientists, never questioned by the less well-
informed multitude for whom science is a religion.

The first of those beautiful illuminated books in which Blake
published his prophetic writings (works no less sacred and inspired
than those Missals and Books of Hours which they resemble) was
a little tractate entitled *There is No Natural Religion*. This is
Blake's carefully argued answer to Locke and his view of human
knowledge as given in the first book of his *Essay concerning
Humane Understanding*. Blake summarises Locke's argument in
his own words: 'Man has no notion of moral fitness but from
Education. Naturally he is only a natural organ subject to Sense.'
This view many would still accept as self-evident. Blake then
takes Locke's premise and exposes its fallacy step by step. Since

it is granted that 'Man cannot naturally Perceive but through his natural or bodily organs' – as Locke had argued – he can only compare and judge what he has so perceived, collecting more and more sense-data, as a computer might by programmed with information, without becoming any the wiser.

> If the many become the same as the few when possess'd.
> More! More! is the cry of the mistaken soul; less than All
> cannot satisfy Man.   (K. 97)

It is Locke and the scientists who cry 'More! More!' and ransack nature from the solar system to the minute structure of cells to add information to information. But their universe is merely quantitative. Like that of 'science fiction', it is, inevitably, claustrophobic because it lacks any vertical dimension in regions of experience other than that of the sensible order. Whether expanded or contracted, by change of scale or the postulation of additional senses, man becomes wearied of 'the same dull round, even of a universe' when that universe is only the 'mill with complicated wheels' of Newtonian science in which we are still, more or less, living to this day.

But because we are not computors programmed with sense-data, 'the desire of Man being infinite, the possession is Infinite & himself Infinite.' The 'true man' is not the mortal body but the life, the consciousness that informs it, the imagination that experiences, not the senses that transmit information. 'The true faculty of knowing must be the faculty that experiences', Blake declares, cutting through all Locke's irrelevances about senses finer or more acute, more or less numerous. 'This faculty I treat of', and indeed throughout his writings he is seeking to communicate his understanding that the 'true man' is the 'Poetic Genius' or 'Imagination', the God within. 'The Poetic Genius is the True Man', and 'As all men are alike in outward form so (and with the same infinite variety) all are alike in the Poetic Genius.' He was seeking for a term to describe the living Self which experiences and understands and creates life.

Blake's tractates against Locke were engraved in 1788; at that time he had not come to use the word Imagination for the indwelling living Self; later he wrote always of 'Jesus, the Imagination'. As 'God made man' he identifies Jesus with the Imagination and in his view Jesus is the Self in all men, fully realised, no doubt in the historical person of the founder of Christianity.

Thomas Taylor the Platonist, the first translator of Plato into English was himself another impassioned opponent of the mechanical philosophy and equalled Blake in his contempt for Locke. He contrasts with Plato's view of ideas as 'eternal and immaterial beings, the originals of all sensible forms,' Locke's opinion that 'ideas are formed from sensible particulars, by a kind of mechanical operation':

> According to Mr. Locke, the soul is a mere *rasa tabula*, an empty recipient, a mechanical blank. According to Plato, she is an ever-written tablet, a plenitude of forms, a vital and intellectual energy. On the former system she is on a level with the most degraded natures, the receptable of material species, and the spectator of delusion and non-entity.

How different, therefore, is Blake's conception of a new-born child from that of Locke and the Behaviourists. [For Blake every child is a divine child, a manifestation of the Imagination of God in the human world.] The birth of Jesus Christ is reflected in every birth. The one God is reflected 'multitudinous' in all the many births which bring the divine Self into human existence. In every child born there lives the indivisible universal 'spirit that knoweth all things'. This is the 'All' that can, in Blake's words, alone satisfy man. The many belongs to the temporal world; in the spiritual world each being experiences the One, not a part of the One (for God is indivisible) but the everywhere presence of the All.

Near the end of his life Blake wrote annotations in his copy of Berkeley's *Siris*; Berkeley the philosopher who had himself answered Locke, and from whom in all likelihood Blake had borrowed some of his own arguments. Blake's marginalia are radiant affirmations of all that he had proclaimed thirty years before in his early tractate: 'Imagination is the Divine Body in Every Man'; 'The Four Senses are the Four Faces of Man & the Four Rivers of the Water of Life.'; and he is still speaking of the Imagination when he writes 'Knowledge is not by deduction, but Immediate by Perception or Sense at once. Christ addresses himself to the Man, not to his Reason.' 'Jesus supposes every

Thing to be Evident to the Child & to the Poor & Unlearned.'
And Blake quotes from the Gospel the text in which it is said
that 'the Spiritual Body or Angel as little Children always behold
the Face of the Heavenly Father.' (K. 774)

And with a final thrust at Locke, 'the Natural Body is an
Obstruction to the Soul or Spiritual Body.' 'What Jesus came to
remove was the Heathen or Platonic Philosophy which blinds the
Eye of Imagination, The Real Man. 'Sense is the Eye of Imagination' (K. 773–5); and to Blake it was clear that a window does
not see; Locke had mistaken the window for the dweller in the
house of the body. But Blake wrote, 'I question not my Corporeal
or Vegetative Eye any more than I would Question a Window
concerning a Sight. I look thro' it & not with it.' (K. 617) And
in verse,

> We are led to Believe a Lie
> When we see With not Thro' the Eye
> Which was Born in a Night to perish in a Night
> (K. 433)

Such is the background of the profound issue which for Blake
underlay the writing of *Songs of Innocence*. The new-born child
is not the poor unformed dough that it seemed to Locke but an
immortal spirit alighting on the threshold of this world, in full
possession of a spiritual identity, no less fully human than a
mature man. In *Infant Joy*, (a poem he illustrated most beautifully with a crimson flower opening to show a new-born infant
in the care of a little female spirit of vegetation) Blake, as nearly
as it is possible for any poet, defines the nature, the essence of
being itself:

> 'I have no name:
> I am but two days old.'
> What shall I call thee?
> 'I happy am,
> 'Joy is my name.'
> Sweet joy befall thee!
> (K. 118)

Being – consciousness – bliss; *sat-chit-ananda;* such was Blake's
understanding of the essence of life. Joy is not something that
happens to the soul, it is the essential nature of every soul.

In the beautiful *Book of Thel* the virgin Thel, who is the ungenerated soul looking down into the world of generation, sees 'the worm upon its dewy bed', an 'image of weakness'. In astonishment she says,

> Art thou but a worm? Image of weakness, art thou but a worm?
> I see thee like an infant wrapped in the lilly's leaf.
>
> (K. 129)

But that worm is the *multum in parvule* of the Christian Nativity.

There were other influences besides Locke who played their part in causing Blake to write *Songs of Innocence*. One of his friends was Johnson, a radical publisher and bookseller in St Paul's Churchyard, for whom Blake worked from time to time as an engraver. Johnson's French editorial assistant was Mary Wollstonecraft who had come under the influence of Rousseau; whom Blake had also read. Rousseau had a view of childhood very different from that of Locke. He believed in the innate goodness of all creatures, according to their nature. No one is born with a bad nature, and Rousseau held the humane and reasonable view that the innate qualities of every child, various as these are, can all be developed in such a way that they will flower of their own accord; just as a flower will develop from its seed if it is given conditions to suit it. This enlightened and kind psychology seems at this time almost self-evident; but this was far from being so in a world where on the one hand Locke and his followers saw a child as a mechanism to be programmed, and on the other the Calvinists taught the terrible doctrine of Predestination. This virtually means that some people are born bad, and destined to damnation. This was the doctrine taught by the Presbyterian Church of Scotland, and there were plenty of Calvinists in England also and in other Protestant countries of Europe.

But infancy, as Blake understood long before Freud, is amoral, governed by the 'pleasure principle.':

> Infancy! fearless, lustful, happy, nestling for delight
> In laps of pleasure: Innocence! honest, open, seeking
> The vigorous joys of morning light; open to virgin bliss.
> Who taught thee modesty, subtil modesty, child of night & sleep?
>
> (K. 193)

Blake wrote no more terrible indictment of the tyranny of morality over the innocent pleasure-principle of childhood than 'A Little Boy Lost,' in *Songs of Experience*. Calvin's Geneva had appalled Shakespeare; but the spirit which had burned a little boy for disrespect towards his father still, Blake reminds us, continues; if not physically, children may still be mentally and spiritually seared and destroyed. People seldom do harm to children from conscious and deliberate sadism, but most often in the name of some false ideology, believing that faults must be corrected and virtues instilled.

W. B. Yeats, in 'A Prayer for my Daughter,' writes of how the soul recovers 'radical innocence':

> And learns that it is self-delighting
> Self-appeasing, self-affrighting,
> And that is own sweet will is Heaven's will.

He is following Blake, who wrote *A Little Boy Lost*.

> Nought loves another as itself
> Nor venerates another so,
> Nor is it possible for Thought
> A greater than itself to know:
>
> And Father, how can I love you
> Or any of my brothers more?
> I love you like the little bird
> That picks up crumbs around the door.
>
> The Priest sat by and heard the child,
> In trembling zeal he seiz'd his hair:
> He led him by his little coat,
> And all admir'd the Priestly care.
>
> And standing on the altar high,
> "Lo! what a fiend is here!" said he,
> "One who sets reason up for judge
> Of our most holy Mystery."
>
> The weeping child could not be heard,
> The weeping parents wept in vain;
> They strip'd him to his little shirt,
> And bound him in an iron chain;

And burn'd him in a holy place
Where many had been burn'd before;
The weeping parents wept in vain.
Are such things done on Albion's shore?

(K. 218–9)

Rousseau's novel ideas on natural goodness were adopted with enthusiasm by Mary Wollstonecraft, and also by Blake, even though the Rousseaunian conception of freedom, being atheist, is only in certain respects comparable with Blake's. Rousseau too believed in an innate principle, and so far the two are alike; but he assigned its operation to the natural and not to the spiritual man. While seeing sympathetically the generosity of impulse which prompted the Swiss reformer, Blake points to the fallacy contained in the use of the word 'liberty' by the ideologists of the French revolution:

Many Persons, such as Pain and Voltaire, with some of the Ancient Greeks, say: 'we will not converse concerning Good and Evil; we will live in Paradise and Liberty.' You may do so in Spirit, but not in the Mortal Body as you pretend. (K. 615–16)

Mary interested herself in questions of education. She translated a charming book entitled *Elements of Morality for the Use of Parents and Children*, by Saltzmann; kindly stories with a great number of illustrations of which Blake made some of the engravings. Mary wrote a book of her own, *Original Stories from Real Life*, for which Blake was both illustrator and engraver. At the time he must have known Mary Wollstonecraft well. *Visions of the Daughters of Albion*, whose theme is the situation of women under restrictive marriage-laws, may also have been inspired by Mary, who as well as publishing her *Vindication of the Rights of Women* adopted Rousseau's views on free love and courageously and disastrously put those ideas into practice. She was abandoned by her lover, the American explorer Imlay, the father of her first daughter, Fanny. Mary afterwards married Godwin, who was also an acquaintance of Blake's, and Shelley's second wife, (Mary also) was the child of this marriage. Shelley was thus in a sense a spiritual heir to Blake's views on love and marriage also.

Blake's *Songs of Innocence* may well have been directly or indirectly suggested to him by Mary Wollstonecraft; they were his contribution to the current conflict of ideas in the field of education at the end of the eighteenth century, and to the new thought of which Rousseau was the moving spirit. His poem *The Schoolboy* well describes the restrictive kind of education practised by those who, believing that all knowledge comes from without, set themselves, to form the infant mind by cramming it with facts. Blake's poem puts forward the view he shared with Mary and with Rousseau that every child will develop by the light of its own nature if given freedom to follow its innate bent. Blake's poem challenges the practice of 'forming' the young mind by loading it with information, envisaging just such a childhood as Wordsworth had been living only a few years earlier, and about which he too, in *The Prelude*, was to write under the influence of Rousseau.

> I love to rise in a summer morn
> When the birds sing on every tree;
> The distant huntsman winds his horn,
> And the sky-lark sings with me.
> Oh! what sweet company.

> But to go to school on a summer morn,
> O! it drives all joy away;
> Under a cruel eye outworn
> The little ones spend the day
> In sighing and dismay.

> Ah! then at times I drooping sit,
> And spend many an anxious hour,
> Nor sit in learning's bower,
> Worn thro' with the dreary shower.

> How can the bird that is born for joy
> Sit in a cage and sing?
> How can a child, when fears annoy,
> But droop his tender wing,
> And forget his youthful spring?

O! father & mother, if buds are nip'd
And blossoms blown away,
And if the tender plants are strip'd
Of their joy in the springing day,
By sorrow and care's dismay,

How shall the summer arise in joy,
Or the summer fruits appear?
Or how shall we gather what griefs destroy,
Or bless the mellowing year,
When the blasts of winter appear?

(K. 124)

In *Tiriel*, engraved in the same year as *Songs of Innocence*, Blake describes with indignation the results of the kind of education he rejects in *The Schoolboy*. Tiriel is the victim of the cruel training and forming of a child until he loses his humanity and becomes in turn the blind tyrant of his own children, passing on the evil he had himself suffered. Blake describes the results in bitter anger. The speaker is the old and dying Tiriel, who sees too late that his humanity had been destroyed:

The child springs from the womb; the father ready stands to form
The infant head, while the mother idle plays with her dog on her
couch:
The young bosom is cold for lack of mother's nourishment, & milk,
Is cut off from the weeping mouth: with difficulty & pain
The father forms a whip to rouze the sluggish senses to act
And scourges off all youthful fancies from the new-born man.
Then walks the weak infant in sorrow, compell'd to number footsteps
Upon the sand.

(K. 110)

It is in *Tiriel* that Blake first asked 'Why is one law given to the lion & the patient ox? The 'one law' is the law of the world of Locke and the materialists, which denies the innate disposition of every creature. In contrast with this 'one law' might stand one of Blake's 'Proverbs of Hell', 'No bird soars too high, if he soars with his own wings.'   (K. 151)

Songs of Innocence can be called poems for children and were presumably written as such, although they are also much more. But for Blake children are themselves fully human, capable of understanding at as great a depth as can adults. Certainly children are unaware of many facts, but they can feel, discern qualities of goodness and beauty or evil and ugliness perhaps even better than adults can. In *Jerusalem*, his longest and last Prophetic poem, Blake writes of

. . . the Wonders Divine
Of Human Imagination throughout all the Three Regions immense
Of Childhood, Manhood & Old Age . . .

(K. 746)

These are but 'regions' within a single experience, a single lifetime, none more or less valuable than the other.

Believing as he did that our world is a mental world Blake understood that dreams are also regions of the soul's reality, places of the Imagination. Thus the dream of Tom the chimneysweeper in *Songs of Innocence* is just as real – perhaps more so – than the drab world of his daily labours. The inner freedom of his dream-world enables Tom to face the day happy and inwardly warm as the poor boys get to work with their bags and brushes.

When my mother died I was very young,
And my father sold me while yet my tongue
Could scarcely cry ' 'weep! 'weep! 'weep! 'weep!'
So your chimneys I sweep, & in soot I sleep.

There's little Tom Dacre, who cried when his head,
That curl'd like a lamb's back, was shav'd: so I said
Hush, Tom! never mind it, for when your head's bare
You know that the soot cannot spoil your white hair.

And so he was quiet, & that very night,
As Tom was a-sleeping, he had such a sight!
That thousands of sweepers, Dick, Joe, Ned, & Jack,
Were all of them lock'd up in coffins of black.

And by came an Angel who had a bright key,
And he open'd the coffins & set them all free;
And down a green plain leaping, laughing, they run
And wash in a river, and shine in the Sun.

Then naked & white, all their bags left behind,
They rise upon clouds and sport in the wind,
And the Angel told Tom, if he'd be a good boy,
He'd have God for his father, & never want joy.

And so Tom awoke; and we rose in the dark,
And got with our bags & our brushes to work.
Tho' the morning was cold, Tom was happy & warm;
So if all do their duty they need not fear harm.

(K. 117)

It is destructive rationalism that deprives many of the comfort
their dreams seek to bring them; as in another poem (which he
did not include in *Songs of Innocence and Experience*) Blake
pathetically describes how to the child the Land of Dreams where
he meets his dead mother is 'better far' than 'this Land of
unbelief and fear'; while his father 'could not get to the other
side' where he could have been with her also, had he accepted
the reality of his experience.

O, what Land is the Land of Dreams?
What are its Mountains & what are its Streams?
O Father, I saw my Mother there,
Among the Lillies by waters fair.

Among the Lambs, clothed in white,
She walk'd with her Thomas in sweet delight,
I wept for joy, like a dove I mourn;
O when shall I again return?

Dear Child, I also by pleasant Streams
Have wander'd all Night in the Land of Dreams,
But tho' calm & warm the waters wide,
I could not get to the other side.

Father, O Father! what do we here
In this Land of unbelief & fear?
The Land of Dreams is better far,
Above the light of the Morning Star.

(K. 427)

Two poems first included in *Songs of Innocence* but later trans-
ferred to *Songs of Experience* are strange narratives, evidently
belonging to some world of myth or fairy-tale that yet does not
seem to be drawn from any familiar tradition. *The Little Girl
Lost* tells of a girl-child who falls asleep beneath a tree in a
'desart wild'; she is found by the lion-king, who carries her to his
cavern where she continues to live safely among leopards and
tigers; in a plate which accompanies this poem a young woman
is shown among her children; so that we must conclude that the
Little Girl descended into the 'world of generation', where in the
'animal' existence of the embodied soul she gave birth to children.
In the second poem, *The Little Girl Found*, her parents, grief-
stricken, seek for their daughter. The mother in turn meets the
Lion-king, and recognises the king of the 'caverns deep' of the
underworld of generation as 'a spirit arm'd in gold'. He leads the
mother to her child, whom she finds living in safety among the
creatures of the natural creation. The stories are based on the
Greater and Lesser Mysteries of Eleusis; doubtless based on
Thomas Taylor the Platonist's *Dissertation on the Mysteries of
Eleusis and Dionysus.* The poems stand appropriately among
his songs of childhood, as an affirmation of his belief that the
soul that enters the world of generation is already complete in
humanity, existing in an eternal world from which it descends
and to which it will return. To Wordsworth's friend Crabb
Robinson Blake declared his belief that it is nonsensical to talk
(as many Christians do) of an immortality after death if there is
no immortality before birth.

It seems virtually certain that Blake did believe in the
Neoplatonic doctrine of reincarnation. The time-world – the
'cave' of those who enter mortal bodies – he saw as an interrup-
tion of the eternal mode of existence and experience which is
native to our humanity. The body he speaks of always as a
'garment' put on by 'the weary man' when he 'enters his cave';
using the very terms of the Neoplatonists who saw this world as
the true Hades, the grave of those who have 'died' from eternity.
The 'true man' or Imagination is bodiless and immaterial, no less
so here and now than hereafter. Blake understood that we are
already spiritual beings, and therefore immeasurable, boundless,
and not (except through our bodies) confined by times and places.

I spoke earlier of the influence on Blake of the hymn-writer

Isaac Watts. Blake may well have liked the simple metre and language of Watts's *Divine Songs* and agreed that they were suitable for children, for he uses similar metres in some of his own *Songs*; although he also uses far more subtle and lovely lyric forms, more reminiscent of Shakespeare than of Watts, and highly characteristic of his own genius. But he did not like the conventional morals the clergyman sought to inculcate, and saw in Watts one of those instructors who were seeking to 'form' the infant mind according to the wisdom of this world. Blake saw the current religious mentality of his day as no less materialist than Locke and Newton. Deism, or 'natural religion', was Blake's abomination. He saw the Deists as really accepting current scientific opinion on the nature of the world, and merely adorning a materialist ideology with morality and meaningless promises of immortality. Blake understood that eternity and immortality are not for the mortal body, but belong to the spirit. Man is eternal and beyond time and space here and now, in the spirit, or not at all. But conventional religion had become such a profane mixture of materialism and credulity that it had nothing to offer those deprived of a truly spiritual religion which, far from being other-worldly, can enable those who understand the true nature of things to live, as Blake did, here and now 'in eternity's sunrise.' There were plenty of other issues on which Blake differed from Watts, and a number of Blake's songs are in answer to Watts's. There is for example a poem entitled *Praise for the Gospel* which no doubt many people in all good faith found acceptable. Indeed it is only recently that the assumption that because Christianity is a true religion all others are therefore false began to be questioned within either the Catholic or the Protestant churches. Watts wrote

> Lord, I ascribe it to thy Grace
> And not to Chance, as others do,
> That I was born of *Christian* race
> And not a *Heathen* or a *Jew*.

Blake, who believed that all religions are one, replied to Watts in a glorious poem which would not have been acceptable in the churches of his own time, 'The Divine Image'.

And all must love the human form,
In heathen, turk, or jew;
Where Mercy, Love, & Pity dwell
There God is dwelling too.

(K. 117)

One of Watts's most popular pieces is *The Sluggard*, (*Moral Songs* No. 1) a poem intended to inculcate the moral virtuousness of hard work. Watts's sluggard refuses to work and asks for

A little more Sleep, and a little more Slumber,
Thus he wastes half his Days, and his Hours without Number.

But in Blake it is the false nurse of the world of Experience who preaches to her charges the morality of Watts, 'Your spring & your day are wasted in play.' The nurse of *Innocence*, on the contrary, loves to hear her children's laughing voices as they play on the hill until the last moment of the day. Watts's sluggard, because he is not industrious, has his garden full of weeds:

I passed by his Garden, and saw the wild Bryar,
The Thorn and the Thistle grow broader and higher;

but Blake's Garden of Love becomes full of thorns because joyless moralists kill the flowers of delight:

And Priests in black gowns were walking their rounds,
And binding with briars my joys & desires.

(K. 215)

Watts's sluggard is a character after Blake's own heart;

He told me his Dreams, talk'd of Eating and Drinking
But he scarce reads his Bible, and never loves Thinking.
Said I then to my Heart, *Here's a Lesson for me*,
That Man's but a Picture of what I might be.
But thanks to my Friends for their Care in my Breeding
Who taught me betimes to love Working and Reading.

As for those friends who teach the child 'betimes to love working and reading', to Blake these are not as Watts supposed, improving, but destroying the young life. If the buds of life have been nipped and the joys stripped from childhood there will be no harvest. Blake's innocents tell their dreams, like Tom the chimney-sweeper; his schoolboy would rather play than work; indeed there is nothing whatever about work in Songs of Innocence, only life itself, with its everlasting play. Eating and drinking too are among the delights of innocence, from 'the table where cherries and nuts are spread.' Watts would surely have reproved the levity of Blake's *Laughing Song*, whose children are as thoughtless as the proverbial grasshopper.

> When the green woods laugh with the voice of joy,
> And the dimpling stream runs laughing by;
> When the air does laugh with our merry wit,
> And the green hill laughs with the noise of it;
>
> When the meadows laugh with lively green,
> And the grasshopper laughs in the merry scene,
> When Mary and Susan and Emily
> With their sweet round mouths sing 'Ha, Ha, He!'
>
> When the painted birds laugh in the shade,
> Where our table with cherries and nuts is spread,
> Come live & be merry, and join with me,
> To sing the sweet chorus of 'Ha, Ha, He!'
>
> (K. 124)

One of Blake's most beautiful images is of that idle creature the grasshopper, conventionally contrasted with the parsimonious ant. Blake, who believed that eternity is ever-present, does not condemn the grasshopper for living in it:

> . . . the Grasshopper that sings & laughs & drinks:
> Winter comes, he folds his slender bones without a murmur
> (K. 513)

And how different is Blake's ant from Watts's models of toiling industry. The hymn-writer cannot have read Jesus's words about taking no thought for the morrow when he praised the ants:

> They don't wear their time out in sleeping and play
> But gather up corn in a sun-shiny day,
>   And for winter they lay up their stores:
> They manage their work in such regular forms
> One would think they foresaw all the frost and the storms.

But Blake saw in these anxious ants, unable to enjoy the sunshine because they are for ever taking thought for the morrow only pathos. He wrote his poem *A Dream* to comfort the anxious with the knowledge that there is a 'watchman of the night' who cares for them.

Once a dream did weave a shade
O'er my Angel-guarded bed,
That an Emmet lost its way
Where on grass me thought I lay.

Troubled, 'wilder'd, and forlorn,
Dark, benighted, travel-worn,
Over many a tangled spray,
All heart-broke I heard her say:

O, my children! do they cry?
Do they hear their father sigh?
Now they look abroad to see:
Now return and weep for me.

Pitying, I drop'd a tear;
But I saw a glow-worm near,
Who replied: What wailing wight
Calls the watchman of the night?

I am set to light the ground
While the beetle goes his round;
Follow now the beetle's hum,
Little wanderer, hie thee home.

(K. 111)

Many have supposed that the state of Innocence is a state of illusion; that the ignorance of childhood must give place to a more 'realistic' view of life which comes with Experience. Some Blake commentators have tried to fit Blake's Innocence and Experience into this preconceived pattern, even suggesting that Blake encountered the stern 'realities' of the world for the first time between the writing of *Songs of Innocence* and *Experience*; a most ridiculous notion, incomparable with his most central teaching on the truth of Imagination and the 'error' of 'creation.' Those who think so have failed to understand that Blake held the paradisal vision to be a vision of reality, while 'Experience' is a false view of the world resulting from the materialist illusion. Experience is not what we learn it is what happens to us when we forget. It is what befalls us when we lose the imaginative vision; or a world of values created by those who do not possess it. This Blake throughout his life tried to make us understand, for he knew that to the majority, in the modern West, the material world is all, and seems the reality, imagination a foolish fancy. But Blake understood that Imagination knows the eternal world; reason, building upon Locke's theory that knowledge comes to us only through the senses, creates its bitter world not by opening but by closing our minds. Blake did not believe, as Wordsworth did, that the 'visionary gleam' belongs only to youth; it is something to be won back, as he had himself kept his vision through a lifetime hard enough by the standards of this world. But to those who knew Blake, the poor engraver, living with his wife in one room, in Fountain Court, off the Strand, seemed like one of the ancient Prophets, walking always with God.

Songs of Experience, then, are all describing states of tragic error and illusion. On the title-page of the book are shown sleepers on a tomb, with mourning figures. The meaning is that those in the world or state of Experience are sleepers, or spiritually dead. The poems are not all about childhood, and few – except *The Tyger* and one or two others – suitable poems for children or written for children. All are concerned with the hells, with the life-destroying results of the world materialism creates in its own image, and which it imposes upon innocence. These states of the human soul are expressed in many situations in the poems. In *Introduction* and *Earth's Answer* Blake goes to the heart of much human misery, the enslavement of sexual love. Selfish and selfless love are contrasted in *The Clod and the Pebble*, the theme of sexual guilt and repression runs through *Nurse's Song, The Sick Rose, The Angel, The Garden of Love*, and *A Little Girl Lost*. Some of the poems are paired with others of the same title or theme in *Songs of Innocence*. To the eyes of Innocence it is a lovely sight to see the orphan children, 'their innocent faces clean' singing in St Paul's on Maundy Thursday;

Seated in companies they sit with radiance all their own.

But without the light of paradise that shines in them they are 'Babes reduc'd to misery/Fed with a cold and usurous hand.' (K. 211) Tom the chimney sweeper is warmed by his dream; but in this world he is 'A little black thing among the snow', treated not as an immortal soul but as a commodity by some master-sweep. *The Little Vagabond* attacks the loveless morality of the churches; *London* is a dark picture of a city whose inhabitants, then as now, come and go, for the most part, unlit by the light of eternity, where the poet can only

> . . . mark in every face I meet
> Marks of weakness, marks of woe.
>   (K. 216)

Infant Sorrow is the lot of countless unloved babes who never are allowed to know 'infant joy'; and *A Little Boy Lost* is sacrificed to parental egoism sheltering itself within the mask of religious virtue. No moral law could be justified that reduced 'Babes to misery'. Blake must have shocked his contemporaries by reminding the religious that 'The Little Vagabond' preferred the 'pleasant and warm' ale house to the cold church, and suggested that 'if at the church they would give us some Ale' things might go better:

> And God, like a father rejoicing to see
> His children as pleasant and happy as he,
> Would have no more quarrel with the Devil or the Barrel,
> But kiss him, and give him both drink and apparel.
>   (K. 216)

It seems that Blake preferred, even for children, any intemperance to temperance sermons. Whereas 'the true man' wears the human face of 'Love, mercy, pity, peace', there is a more terrible image in the world cut off from the 'God within'. This poem Blake entitles *A Divine Image*: for when man does not bear in his soul the signature of God, then he himself invents an image of God in the likeness of his own selfhood:

> Cruelty has a Human Heart
> And Jealousy a Human Face,
> Terror, the Human Form Divine,
> And Secrecy the Human Dress.

The Human Dress is forged Iron
The Human Form a fiery Forge,
The Human Face a Furnace seal'd,
The Human Heart its hungry Gorge.

(K. 221)

This is the terrible image of the God of 'Natural Religion' worshipped by great numbers of human beings who have no experience of the 'God Within'.

There is in *Vala* or *The Four Zoas* a terrible but magnificent description of the state Blake calls Experience; the aspect of this world for those who can discern no other; it is the earth-mother who speaks:

I am made to sow the thistle for wheat, the nettle for a nourishing
dainty.
I have planted a false oath in the earth; it has brought forth a poison
tree.
I have chosen the serpent for a councillor, & the dog
For a schoolmaster to my children,
I have blotted out from light & living the dove & nightingale,
And I have caused the earth worm* to beg from door to door.
I have taught the thief a secret path into the house of the just,
I have taught pale artifice to spread his nets upon the morning.
My heavens are brass, my earth is iron, my moon a clod of clay,
My sun a pestilence burning at noon & a vapour of death in night.
What is the price of Experience? do men buy it for a song?
Or wisdom for a dance in the street? No, it is bought with the price
Of all that a man hath, his house, his wife, his children.
Wisdom is sold in the desolate market where none come to buy,
And in the wither'd field where the farmer plows for bread in vain.

(K. 290)

Blake is not here writing against Political & Social 'Conditions': this is the world into which Adam and Eve are driven, to learn wisdom in the barren land of 'error or creation'. The passage continues with a bitter description of the conditions of poverty and labour to which the Man and Woman were condemned by their fatal choice. But yet, realistic as are his descriptions of the 'conditions' of society in his own city of London, that dark world

(*The 'earth worm' is man seen as the 'mortal worm')

of experience is called a 'deadly dream' into which mankind has fallen; an illusion of those who live not from the 'divine humanity' within, but from the ego, 'the God of this world' of the five senses.

That is why *Songs of Experience* opens and *Innocence* closes with 'the voice of the bard' – the poetic genius who speaks from, and to, the Imagination, 'the true man', calling to the fallen soul of the world to return to the Imagination and to awaken from her 'deadly dream'. The voice of the Bard is the voice of Imagination:

> Hear the voice of the Bard!
> Who Present, Past & Future, sees;
> Whose ears have heard
> The Holy Word
> That walk'd among the ancient trees,
>
> Calling the lapsed Soul,
> And weeping in the evening dew;
> That might controll
> The starry pole,
> And fallen, fallen light renew!
>
> (K. 210)

There could be no clearer answer to those who imagine that Blake thought we could learn anything from what he calls 'experience' than the last poem of *Songs of Innocence*; 'The Voice of the Ancient Bard':

> Youth of delight, come hither,
> And see the opening morn,
> Image of truth new born.
> Doubt is fled, & clouds of reason,
> Dark disputes & artful teazing.
> Folly is an endless maze,
> Tangled roots perplex her ways.
> How many have fallen there!
> They stumble all night over bones of the dead,
> And feel they know not what but care,
> And wish to lead others when they should be led.
>
> (K. 126)

8 *Berkeley, Blake and the New Age*

To set the name of Blake beside that of Berkeley is in itself to remove discussion from the order of philosophy, of which Berkeley was so pure an exponent. To introduce as a third term the apocalyptic concept of a new age must seem an unthinkable degradation of Berkeley's serene thought. But the history of ideas can never be contained within prescribed channels; poets are unscrupulous borrowers from the philosophers, and Blake among English poets the most triumphant animator of abstract thought with the turbulent life of prophetic mythology.

It was Blake who proclaimed a new age; not on his own authority but upon that of Emanuel Swedenborg. Blake was not an original thinker, and the arrows he loosed with such force from his bow of burning gold, though tipped with his own fire, were seldom of his own making. When in his *Marriage of Heaven and Hell* Blake announced 'a new heaven is begun', the prophecy is Swedenborg's; and the new vision of that age is – allowing for common sources within a tradition – Berkeley's philosophy.

Such a sweeping statement may well be challenged, and I must therefore define and set limits to my claim. Blake and Berkeley are alike, it is true, in their total rejection of materialism, their total adherence to the view that mind, or spirit, is the only substantial reality; and both have opposed their arguments to the philosophy of Locke. But does this necessarily mean that Blake knew Berkeley's works, or borrowed from him? Such is the unanimity of the Platonic tradition (using this term in its widest sense to include, besides the works of Plotinus and the Neoplatonists, the Hermetica and the Gnostics, Boehme and Paracelsus and Swedenborg, acknowledged by Blake as his teachers) that it is not always possible to say which particular writer is the source of some common idea.

Blake himself made no acknowledgments to Berkeley, but

then he seldom acknowledged his sources. Blake throve on opposition, and even Swedenborg is named only when Blake is picking a quarrel with him, and not as the source of his innumerable borrowings. When in 1819 Blake annotated his copy of *Siris* his work lay behind him. The marginalia could be read as applications of Berkeley's own arguments as a commentary, or even criticism, of the annotated statements. The last of Blake's marginalia – 'What Jesus came to Remove was the Heathen or Platonic Philosophy, which blinds the Eye of Imagination, The Real Man' (K. 775) – is outrageous when we consider the extent of Blake's borrowings from the Platonists. Perhaps it was that Blake identified himself so completely with the ideas he accepted that they seemed his own; it was only when he differed that he named their authors. Is it for some such reason that the names of Bacon, Newton and Locke occur constantly, while there is no mention of Berkeley?

Such a negative argument of course proves nothing; and unless it can be shown that there is more than a coincidental resemblance between the two great opponents of Locke, the case remains open. However, the similarities are there, and – supposing for a moment that there is a time-spirit whose operation is distinct from the known influence of one mind upon another – we must see Blake as the next leaf upon Berkeley's branch.

Berkeley was perhaps more concerned to avert a New Age than to introduce one; in his *Third Dialogue between Hylas and Philonous* he turns aside the shocking charge of innovation:

But the novelty, Philonous, the novelty! there lies the danger. New notions should always be discountenanced; they unsettle men's minds, and nobody knows where they will end.

The philosopher dismisses so foolish a notion:

Why the materialist concept of matter, a notion that hath no foundation in sense or in reason, or in divine authority, should be thought to unsettle the belief of such opinions as are grounded in all or any of these, I cannot imagine. '*Three Dialogues between Hylas and Philonous*,' *The Works of*

George Berkeley (London: Thomas Nelson and Sons 1953)
II 243. Hereafter cited in the text as B and followed by
volume and page references.

Berkeley shows no inkling of Blake's New Age as the likely outcome of his thought. Far from seeing himself as an innovator
Berkeley's appeal (in *Siris* explicitly) was to 'revealed' tradition,
not limited to the Jewish scriptures. 'In the Timaeus of Plato,' he
wrote, 'mention is made of ancient persons, authors of traditions,
and the offspring of the gods' (B. V. 154); traditions embodied
in 'the Platonic, Pythagorean, Egyptian and Chaldaic philosophy'
(B. VI. 38), and above all in Plotinus and in the Hermetica. The
arguments Berkeley brought to bear with such precision upon
the thought of Newton and Locke are formulated in such a way
as to be a self-consistent appeal to reason; but his premises are
those of the Platonic philosophers. Even if it be argued, from the
absence of reference to their works in his early notebooks, that at
the time of writing his *Principles of Human Knowledge* Berkeley
knew only Plato's own writings, he would have found the essential
teachings there. Everard's translation of *The Divine Pymander
of Hermes Trismegistus* was, however, published in 1650 and
there remains a strong possibility that Berkeley read this work
long before (in *Siris*) he makes direct mention of it. Casaubon's
challenge and Cudworth's defense of the authenticity of this
work brought it into prominence in the latter half of the seventeenth century.

Blake's new age was likewise a return to the same tradition,
which was to become seminal in the Romantic movement.
Coleridge named his first son Berkeley; and Blake made of
Berkeley's creed a manifesto.

Let us consider some of the parallels. In his *Principles of
Human Knowledge* Berkeley rejects the assumption that supposes
'visible objects to be corporeal substances':

For as to what is said of the absolute existence of unthink-
ing things without any relation to their being perceived, that
seems perfectly unintelligible. Their *esse* is *percipi* (B. II.
42); "Natural Phenomena are only natural appearances"
(B. V. 135)

Blake forcefully sums up this philosophy of 'seeing is believing':

> He who Doubts from what he sees
> Will ne'er Believe, do what you Please.
> If the Sun & Moon should doubt,
> They'd immediately Go out.
>   (K. 433)

and in his declaration of faith that accompanies his drawing of the *Laocoon* group Blake wrote:

> All that we See is Vision, from Generated Organs gone as soon as come, Permanent in The Imagination, Consider'd as Nothing by the Natural Man.   (K. 776)

Berkeley, answering the Cartesian view that extension in space constitutes body, writes:

> But though we should grant this unknown substance [matter] may possibly exist, yet where can it be supposed to be? That it exists not in the mind is agreed, and that it exists not in place is no less certain: since all (place or) extension exists only in the mind . . . It remains therefore that it exists nowhere at all.   (B. II. 70)

Blake adds only passion to Berkeley's argument:

> Mental Things are alone Real: what is call'd Corporeal, Nobody knows of its Dwelling Place: it is in Fallacy, & its Existence an Imposture. Where is the Existence Out of Mind or Thought? Where is it but in the Mind of a Fool? (K. 617)

Berkeley illustrates by example:

> It is indeed an opinion strangely prevailing amongst men, that houses, mountains, rivers, and in a word all sensible objects have an existence natural or real, distinct from their being perceived by the understanding   (B. II. 42).

And Blake wings these same images with poetry:

For all are Men in Eternity, Rivers, Mountains, Cities, Villages,
All are Human, & when you enter into their Bosoms you walk
In Heavens & Earths, as in your own Bosom you bear your Heaven
And Earth & all you behold; tho it appears without, it is Within,
In your Imagination, of which this World of Mortality is but a Shadow.

(K. 709)

Again, Berkeley writes:

> We have no proof, either from experiment or reason, of any
> other agent or efficient cause than mind or spirit. When,
> therefore, we speak of corporeal agents or corporeal causes,
> this is to be understood in a different, subordinate, and
> improper sense;   (B. V. 83, *Siris*, p. 154)

that is, in Blake's words,

> . . . every Natural Effect has a Spiritual Cause, and Not
> A Natural; for a Natural Cause only seems . . .
> (K. 513)

Blake's first editor and greatest disciple, himself also prophet
of a new Age, wrote

> . . . God-appointed Berkeley that proved all things a dream,
> That this pragmatical, preposterous pig of a world,
>   its farrow that so solid seem
> Must vanish on the instant if the mind but change its theme.

Yeats would not have called Berkeley 'God-appointed' just
because he was an ordained bishop; rather because he saw in
him the herald of (in Yeats's phrase) 'the rise of soul against
intellect, now beginning in the world.' And what is a new age
if not a change of premises? And with a change of premises a
change of values, in the light of which much current knowledge
becomes irrelevant, and much excluded knowledge is seen to have
a significance formerly overlooked.

The difference between Berkeley's calm challenge to the

philosophy of Bacon, Newton, and Locke and Blake's embattled zeal is that between a declaration of war and war itself. Berkeley had published his *Principles of Human Knowledge*, 'wherein the chief causes of Error and difficulty in the Sciences, with the grounds of Scepticism, Atheism and Irreligion are inquired into' in 1710. (See also *Siris* 331) Blake was born in 1757, and the century that lies between Berkeley's world and Blake's had seen the transition of natural philosophy from the realm of ideas into national life. When Blake described 'Bacon, Newton and Locke' as 'the three great leaders of Atheism, or Satan's doctrine' he too was expressing a rational and not an emotional judgment; for, as he told Crabb Robinson the diarist, 'everything is Atheism which assumes the reality of the natural and unspiritual world.' That is how Satan comes to be among the natural philosophers; but when he wrote that 'the Mills of Satan' 'overshadow'd the whole earth' his protest was, above all, that an ideology was gaining domination and changing the quality of life. Blake wrote his poem *Milton* – his own version of the causes of the loss of Paradise – in order to identify the true Satan as the mechanistic philosophy:

> For Bacon & Newton, sheath'd in dismal steel, their terrors hang
> Like iron scourges over Albion . . .
>
> (K. 635)

For Blake there were no opinions, ideas, theories, philosophies as distinct from human beings possessed by, and in their lives giving expression to, these ideas; no pure reason, but a rational state of mind – that state he personifies in the usurping gray-bearded tyrant Urizen, cold, blind, anxious, cruel personification of the abstract reasoner. He understood that ideas, like passions, cannot otherwise exist than in men; and for Blake the final test of any philosophy is the kind of human beings it produces. He saw about him in London, and in Europe also, men possessed by 'the notions of external existence, necessity and fate' (B. V. 127) loosed upon the world by the mechanical and geometrical philosophers. Blake saw the materialist philosophy not as one amongst other hypotheses all as harmless as poisons in glass cases, but as a spiritual sickness, 'the sickness of Albion,' the national being of England; and this mortal sickness is the theme of his longest prophetic poem, *Jerusalem*, and in various aspects of virtually the whole of his work. Nothing – and Blake saw this not as a remote possibility but as the actual condition of multitudes of human beings – could be more terrible than the situation of living spirits in a supposedly lifeless and indifferent universe, subject to Newton's great mechanism of time, space and inanimate matter operating autonomously, outside mind and thought. What is in natural space has only quantity and dimension. What is in mind is a living experience of the beholder; it has meaning and quality. Sun, moon and stars are to a scientist (insofar as he is watching them from the point of view of science) measurable but lifeless phenomena whose quantitative immensities reduce man to a speck of dust powerless in an indifferent universe. To free 'enslaved' humanity from the false concepts of the natural philosophers was Blake's prophetic task; to summon Albion

> To bathe in the Waters of life, to wash off the Not Human . . .
> To cast off Bacon, Locke & Newton from Albion's covering.
>
> (K. 533)

Not that Blake supposed the materialist philosophers to have any ill intent; on the contrary, the disastrous consequences, in human terms, of their search for truth were neither intended nor foreseen by its agents. Blake writes of Satan's 'self-imposition.' (Satan is 'the Mind of the Natural Frame').

> Seeming a brother, being a tyrant, even thinking himself a brother
> While he is murdering the just: prophetic I behold
> His future course thro' darkness and despair to eternal death.
>
> (K. 487)

Big Brother indeed! The Big Brother of materialist philosophy must of necessity become a tyrant because he compels humanity (in Yeats's words) to become passive before a mechanized nature, until, as Blake says, 'his machines are woven with his life.'

Many readers of Blake must have wondered why 'Satan's Tyranny' should be defined not in moral terms but in terms of Newtonian science: '. . . Satan's Mathematic Holiness, Length, Bredth & Highth' (K. 521). But Blake was in truth going to the heart of the matter, as Berkeley before him. The building of a lifeless universe outside mind and thought, the imposition of a reign of quantity upon immeasurable life, is, as Blake understood, the supreme blasphemy against the God of life and crime against man. Newtonian space

> . . . shrinks The Organs
> Of Life till they become Finite and itself seems Infinite.

Berkeley was no mystic; indeed, his world is essentially concrete, particular, picturable, existential. So far was he from teaching the 'unreality' of the sensible world – as has been said of him by his opponents – that he turns the tables on poor Hylas who, deprived of the comforting concept of 'matter', feels as if the ground had been taken from under his feet in a most literal sense. The philosopher replies:

> I am of a vulgar cast, simple enough to believe my senses, and leave things as I find them. To be plain, it is my opinion that the real things are those very things I see and feel and perceive by my senses.   (B. II. 229)

There is a pleasant eighteenth-century coolness in Berkeley's immaterialism, a world away from Blake's impassioned defense of essentially the same point of view in a letter to an unimaginative patron who had complained that his work was too visionary. To which Blake replied by insisting, like Berkeley, that his is the real world as it appears to the senses:

> I know that This World Is a World of imagination & Vision. I see Every thing I paint In This World, but Every body does not see alike . . . To the Eyes of the Man of Imagination. Nature is Imagination itself. As a man is, So he Sees. As the Eye is formed, such are its Powers. You certainly Mistake, when you say that the Visions of Fancy are not to be found in This World. To Me This World is all One continued Vision of Fancy or Imagination.   (K. 793)

To be a visionary is not to see a different world from others, but to see the same world differently. The world of 'Newton's Pantocrator' Blake calls 'cruel' because it is a mechanism indifferent to life; it is 'outside eternity', 'the void outside existence.'

'this soul-shuddering vacuum,' 'the petrific, abominable chaos,' 'the world of eternal death.' The living mind, by contrast, Blake calls a world of 'eternal birth' because everything perceived is new-created every moment we behold it, free from the restrictive limits of time and space, not subject to decay or death. Outside the perceiving mind, in the wilderness of corporeal space, how, he asks, are

How are Beasts & Birds & Fishes & Plants & Minerals
Here fix'd into a frozen bulk subject to decay & death?
Those Visions of Human Life & Shadows of Wisdom & Knowledge
Are here frozen to unexpansive deadly destroying terrors.

(K. 525)

And the poet laments that in the world of quantity

. . . A Rock, a Cloud, a Mountain,
Were now not vocal, as in Climes of happy Eternity,
Where the lamb replies to the infant voice, the lion to the man of
years,
Giving them sweet instructions; where the Cloud, the River & the
Field
Talk with the husbandman & shepherd . . .

(K. 315)

For Berkeley too the phenomena give 'sweet instructions' and have meaning as well as beauty. In the margin of his copy of *Siris* Blake wrote, 'knowledge is not by deduction, but Immediate by Perception or Sense at once' (K. 774); and this may be read as a just paraphrase of Berkeley who on an earlier page of the same book had written:

The phenomena of nature which strike on the senses and are understood by the mind, form not only a magnificent spectacle, but also a most coherent, entertaining, and instructive Discourse . . . conducted, adjusted and ranged by the greatest wisdom   (B. V. 121)

The order we perceive in the phenomena, their meaning, and also their beauty, is the order, meaning and beauty of a living mind. It is, according to Blake, the Newtonian philosophy.

Which separated the stars from the mountains, the mountains from
Man,
And left Man, a little grovelling Root outside of Himself.

(K. 639)

Locke had argued that the creatures are conditioned through the
sense; for Blake they are activated from 'within,' each creature
a unique expression of ever-various life. Differences between
the creatures are accounted for, by Locke, by differences of the
sense-organs. Locke accepted the doctrine of a 'great chain of
being' – a well-established concept which he would have to meet
if he were to make his philosophy credible.

> Imagine that Spirits can assume to themselves Bodies of
> different Bulk, Figure, and Conformation of Parts. Whether
> one great advantage some of them may have over us, may
> not lie in this, that they can so frame, and shape to them-
> selves Organs of Sensation or Perception, as to suit their
> present Design, and the Circumstances of the Object they
> would consider. For how much would that Man exceed all
> others in Knowledge, who had the Faculty so to alter the
> Structure of his Eyes, that one Sense, as to make it capable
> of all the several degrees of Vision which the assistance of
> Glasses . . . has taught us to conceive. (John Locke, *Essay
> Concerning Human Understanding* (London, 1690), Book
> II, Ch. 23, para. 13, p. 141. Hereafter cited as HU and
> followed by book, and page references.

Size is a special case of the possible worlds Locke postulates,
vividly brought to the notice of philosophers by the invention of
the microscope:

> Nay, if that most instructive of our Senses, Seeing, were in
> any man 1000 or 100000 (times) more acute than it is now
> by the best Microscope, things several millions of Times less
> than the smallest Object of his Sight now, would then be
> visible to his naked Eyes . . . But then he would be in a
> quite different World from other People . . . (HU, II, 23 : 12,
> p. 140)

Blake seems to be paraphrasing Locke's picture of possible worlds in Bromion's speech on the uses of the microscope.

> Thou knowest that the ancient trees seen by thine eyes have fruit

'The ancient trees' is a phrase used elsewhere by Blake to signify the 'garden of Eden', the natural world God made for man.

> But knowest thou that trees and fruits flourish upon the earth
> To gratify senses unknown? trees, beasts and birds unknown,
> Unknown, not unperceiv'd, spread in the infinite microscope,
> In places yet unvisited by the voyager, and in worlds
> Over another kind of seas, and in atmospheres unknown
>
> (K. 192)

This is the world of 'science fiction', the materialist's universe basically unchanged but spatially extended, with an ad. lib. addition of new phenomena. Locke's multiplication whether of senses or of phenomena adds nothing but 'More! More!' Was Blake following Berkeley in setting against the 'One law for lion and ox' the infinite variety and richness of innate ideas:

> With what sense is it that the chicken shuns the ravenous hawk?
> With what sense does the tame pigeon measure out the expanse?
> With what sense does the bee form cells? have not the mouse & frog
> Eyes and ears and sense of touch? Yet are their habitations
> And their pursuits as different as their forms and as their joys.
> Ask the wild ass why he refuses burdens, and the meek camel
> Why he loves man: is it because of eye, ear, mouth, or sense of touch
> Or breathing nostrils? No, for these the wolf and tyger have . . .
>
> (K. 191)

Living existence is immeasurable and infinitely various, and every creature follows the inner law of its own being:

> The sea fowl takes the wintry blast for a covering for her limbs,
> And the wild snake the pestilence to adorn him with gems & gold;
> And trees & birds & beasts & men behold their eternal joy.
> Arise, you little glancing wings, and sing your infant joy!
> Arise, and drink your bliss, for everything that lives is holy!
>
> (K. 195)

The joy of each creature – and Blake extends his arguments to human life – is the innate law of each living spirit. 'Life delights in life.'

It is not my intention to present in detail the arguments of Locke on the nature of perception, or Berkeley's answers to these, nor to evaluate Blake's contribution to the discussion, viewed as philosophy. Blake was impatient of the steps of argument, often certainly because he had already arrived on the wings of intuition at a realization of the term. However, it is tempting to conclude that Blake read Berkeley's dismissal of Locke's argument that we could know more of an object by possessing more senses. We should be no nearer to seeing a material object because however acute our senses, 'it is the mind that frames all that variety of bodies which compose the visible world, any one whereof does not exist any longer than it is perceived.' For Berkeley there is no 'object' other than the ever-fluctuating series of appearances. And Blake,

> If Perceptive Organs vary, Objects of Perception seem to vary:
> If the Perceptive Organs close, their Objects seem to close also.
>
> (K. 661)

Berkeley argues that 'at length, after various changes of size and shape, when the sense becomes infinitely acute, the body shall seem infinite'. (B. II. 60) Doubtless the philosopher was considering infinity as the logical term of his argument. Was Blake fired by Berkeley's word, 'infinite', when in *There is no Natural Religion* he wrote,

> The desire of Man being Infinite, the possession is Infinite & himself Infinite.   (K. 97)

– and two years later, in the *Marriage of Heaven and Hell*,

> . . . the whole creation will be consumed and appear infinite and holy, whereas it now appears finite and corrupt . . . If the doors of perception were cleansed everything would appear to man as it is, infinite.   (K. 154)

What in Berkeley is a philosophical demonstration becomes in Blake a mystical affirmation. For Blake one thing alone is holy – being, consciousness, bliss – life itself.

The nature of the perceptible world is central to Blake's prophetic vision. He returns to the attack again and again. In his poem *Europe* Berkeley's theme is introduced by a fairy in a 'streaked tulip', the same flower the philosopher had chosen, in his Third Dialogue, to illustrate, one May morning, that *esse* is *percipi*. Blake puts to this Berkeleyan fairy the great question,

> Then tell me, what is the material world, and is it dead?

– to which the living spirit of the flower replies to the poet,

> I'll . . . shew you all alive
> The world, where every particle of dust breathes forth its joy.
>
> (K. 237)

The fairy goes on to lecture Blake about the five senses in an expanded version of the aphorism in the *Marriage of Heaven and Hell*, 'For man has closed himself up, till he sees all things thro' narrow chinks of his cavern'. (K. 154) Locke too had used this image of Plato's when he defined the senses as 'the windows by which light is let into this dark room'; 'For, (he continues) methinks the Understanding is not much unlike a closet, wholly shut from the light, with only some little openings left to let in external visible resemblances'. (HU. II. 17) Blake's use of the plural – 'chinks' – seems to suggest that Locke is his primary source in this instance. To the five senses as the causes of exclusion rather than of admission Blake returns again and again, in a passage repeated, with slight variations:

> Ah weak & wide astray! Ah shut in narrow doleful form,
> Creeping in reptile flesh upon the bosom of the ground!
> The Eye of Man a little narrow orb, clos'd up & dark,
> Scarcely beholding the great light, conversing with the Void;
> The Ear a little shell, in small volutions shutting out
> All melodies . . .
>
> (K. 484)

In one of the early Lambeth poems, *The Song of Los*, Blake paraphrases Ovid's metamorphosis of Cadmus and Harmonia into serpents. Blake's ancestral figures, Har and Heva are, like them, changed into serpents by the 'shrinking' of their senses:

> . . . they shrunk
> Into two narrow doleful forms
> Creeping in reptile flesh upon
> The bosom of the ground;
> And all the vast of Nature shrunk
> Before their shrunken eyes.
>
> (K. 246)

Lest we should miss his meaning, Blake specifies the 'laws' which were to bind Har and Heva

> . . . more
> And more to Earth, Closing & restraining
> Till a Philosophy of Five Senses was complete.
> Urizen wept & gave it into the hands of Newton & Locke
>
> (K. 246)

This 'shrinking' recurs in Blake's last poem, *Jerusalem*:

> . . . as their eye & ear shrunk, the heavens shrunk away:
> . . .
> Afar into the unknown night the mountains fled away . . .
>
> (K. 702)

> . . . and the Sun is shrunk; the Heavens are shrunk
> Away into the far remote, & the Trees & Mountains wither'd
>
> (K. 703)

In the *Book of Urizen* also the shrinking into reptile-form is described, with an additional image, that of the seven days of creation; Blake is writing of Urizen's victims:

> Six days they shrank up from existence,
> And on the seventh day they rested,
> And they blessed the seventh day in sick hope,
> And forgot their eternal life.
>
> (K. 236)

The seventh day is blessed because it sets a limit to the Fall. The seven days of creation here correspond to changes in man himself; and for this unusual reading of the Mosaic myth Blake seems to have drawn upon Berkeley; for it is most unlikely that he could have hit upon the idea himself (or found it in

Malebranche, who may have been Berkeley's source). In this strange account of the creation, as a series of changes in the perceiving mind, appearing in several versions in the early Lambeth books, we surely have evidence of Blake's knowledge of Berkeley's writings, and not merely of Berkeley's sources. In the third *Dialogue*, Hylas brings out his trump card against the Immaterialist philosophy:

> *Hylas*: The Scripture account of the Creation, is what appears to be utterly irreconcilable with your notions. Moses tells us of a Creation: a Creation of what? Of ideas? No certainly, but of things, of real things, solid corporeal substances . . .

To which the philosopher replies:

> Moses mentions the sun, moon and stars, earth and sea, plants and animals: that all these do really exist, and were in the beginning created by God, I make no question. If by *ideas* you mean immediate objects of understanding, or sensible things which cannot exist unperceived, or out of a mind, then these things are ideas . . . the Creation therefore I allow to have been a creation of things, of *real* things . . . But as for solid corporeal substances, I desire you to show me where Moses makes mention of them . . . I imagine that if I had been present at the Creation, I should have seen things produced into being, that is, become perceptible, in the order described by the sacred historian. (B. II. 250–1)

Blake distinguished between infinite and finite perception and relates the creation only to the latter.

> Many suppose that before the Creation All was Solitude & Chaos. This is the most pernicious Idea that can enter the Mind, as it . . . Limits All Existence to Creation & Chaos, To the Time & Space fixed by the Corporeal Vegetative Eye . . . Eternity Exists, and All things in Eternity, Independent of Creation . . . (K. 614)

He called the creator of this world, a 'very cruel being,' contrasting the temporal creation with 'the Nature of Eternal Things Display'd, All Springing from the Divine Humanity' (K. 612). Temporal creation is of course illusory; real existence is in mind. 'Vision or Imagination,' he says, 'is a Representation of what Eternally Exists, Really & Unchangeably' (K. 604). 'Error, or Creation' is an 'empire of nothing,' a fallacy of 'old Nobodaddy,' the rational mind. 'Error, or Creation, will be Burned up & then, & not till Then, Truth or Eternity will appear. It is Burnt up the Moment Men cease to behold it' (K. 617)

Blake's account of the origin of 'Error, or Creation' is repeated three times in his Prophetic Books as the myth of the 'binding of Urizen,' the rational faculty. The seven 'ages' of creation are changes in the consciousness from infinite to finite perception. First the brain is 'roofed over' – the first stage imprisoning of 'the caverned man' within the world of the ratio. Blake leaves us in no doubt as to how he regarded this process; at the end of the first day of creation,' . . . a first Age passed over, /And a state of dismal woe.' Next the heart sinks into the abyss of outer creation, 'And a second Age passed over, /And a state of dismal woe.' The eyes, closed in 'two little caves,' 'beheld the deep'; the ears, the nostrils, the tongue of hunger and thirst'; and last, the arms are outstretched into corporeal space, and the feet of man 'stamp'd the nether Abyss.' This is the term of creation,

> And now his eternal life
> Like a dream was obliterated.
> (K. 228–30)

There are echoes of this theme in the lament of Oothoon, the generated soul:

They told me that I had five senses to inclose me up,
And they inclos'd my infinite brain into a narrow circle,
And sunk my heart into the Abyss, a red, round globe, hot burning,
Till all from life I was obliterated and erased.

(K. 191)

In yet another symbolic figure Blake endeavours to make clear what was for him so vital an issue. The mental nature of the phenomenal world was not for him, as perhaps for Berkeley, a matter of correct thinking, but of our living experience of the earth. He constructed a *mandala* (in C. G. Jung's sense of a geometrical representation of the psyche) and 'Golgonooza' – Blake's uncouth name for the interior city of Albion 'The Spiritual Fourfold London' – is, like St John's Heavenly Jerusalem, a structure, with four 'gates,' towards each of the cardinal points. Like Blake's 'four Zoas' the 'gates' of Golgonooza correspond to Jung's four 'functions' of the psyche: reason, feeling, intuition and sensation. In the Biblical story of the Fall, it is the closing of the gate of Eden that banishes mankind from the Earthly Paradise into a desolate and barren land. Blake interprets this as the externalization of the sensible world, for the 'western gate' of the city – the gate of the sense – is closed.

To the majority of Western mankind this exclusion is self-evident; we do not see any problem at all in so obvious an assumption. It is very difficult for us, conditioned as we are, even to conceive of a state of consciousness in which the sensible world might be considered as part of our subjectivity. In the Far East the reverse is the case. In the Indian philosophic traditions, whether Buddhist or Vedantic, it is axiomatic that all we perceive exists in the mind, whereas to us this seems almost inconceivable or is imaginable only by strenuous effort. It is precisely this blockage of consciousness – for as such he saw it – which Blake has represented in his mandala of the closed gate. But in some, Blake says – and he must surely have included Berkeley among these – the 'western gate' is open. He himself claims to be one of these. 'The artist is an inhabitant of that happy country [Eden] and . . . the world of vegetation and generation may expect to be opened again to Heaven, through Eden, as it was in the beginning.' (K. 578) Eden is the phenomenal world, re-entered when it becomes, once more, an aspect of our consciousness, and not a separate and indifferent corporeal order. In *The Marriage of Heaven and Hell* he had written many years before that when the Cherub leaves his guard over Eden's closed gate, 'the notion that man has a body distinct from his soul is to be expunged,' (K. 154) and body is once again known as a 'portion of soul'.

What, then, is the state of consciousness Blake seeks so urgently to describe? When towards the end of his life Blake read – or re-read – *Siris*, he wrote in the margin, 'the Spiritual Body or Angel as little Children always behold the Face of the Heavenly Father' (K. 774). This is Blake's understanding of Berkeley's conception of the sensible world as an immediate action of the mind of God upon consciousness: the world all behold is, in the most literal sense, 'the Face of the Heavenly Father.' Berkeley, with that poetic perception which he occasionally allows to shine through his philosophic discourse, makes his appeal to the nature-poetry of the Old Testament

> which constantly ascribe those effects to the immediate hand of God, that heathen philosophers impute to Nature. *The Lord, he causeth the vapours to ascend; he maketh lightnings with rain; he bringeth the wind out of his treasures. He turneth the shadow of death into the morning, and maketh it soft with showers* . . . (B. II. 109–10)

– and so on. Berkeley, goes so far as to say we can 'see God' since in nature his countenance is everywhere revealed to us:

> . . . we need only open our eyes to see the sovereign Lord of all things . . . every thing we see, hear, feel, or in any wise perceive by sense, being a sign or effect of the Power of God. (B II 108)

In such passages Berkeley seems to be deeply influenced by the Hermetic writers, where many such passages may be found as this from Book X:

> And do you say: 'God is invisible'? Speak not so. Who is more manifest than God? For this very purpose he has made all things, that through all things you may see him. (*Hermetica*, X. 135–6)

Blake reproaches the Reasoner for

> . . . in spaces remote
> Seeking the eternal which is always present to the wise
> (K. 361)

I know of no other English poet who is in this respect so close to the Psalmists as Blake is; for him the phenomena of nature are 'visions of eternity,' and informed by the living presence of living mind. Blake's nature-poetry is in marked contrast with that of Wordsworth, who admired Newton. Blake wrote that 'the abstract Voids between the Stars are the Satanic Wheels' (K. 633) and pleads with his readers

> Seek not thy heavenly father then beyond the skies,
> There Chaos dwells & ancient Night . . .
>
> (K. 502)

If Berkeley's great learning in the Neoplatonic and Hermetic literature gave him the substance of his immaterialism, he had no knowledge of the metaphysical thought closest to his own – the Indian; and in particular the Vedantic concept of 'Ishvara,' the living mind in which the phenomena (Maya) are made manifest. Blake knew the *Bhagavad Geeta* in its first English translation (by Sir Charles Wilkins): and he also seems to have known some of the *Proceedings of the Calcutta Society of Bengal* promoted by Sir William Jones. He it was who pointed out the similarity of Berkeley's thought to that of Vedanta:

> The fundamental tenet of the Vedantic school . . . consisted, not in denying the existence of matter, that is, of solidity, impenetrability and extended figure (to deny which would be lunacy) but, in correcting the popular notion of it, and in contending, that it has no essence independent of mental perception, that existence and perceptibility are convertible terms, that external appearances and sensations are illusory and would vanish into nothing if the divine energy, which alone sustains them, were suspended but for a moment . . . A view which has been maintained in the present century with great elegance, but little public applause. (Sir William Jones. *Works.* III. 229)

Jones's account of the Vedantic conception of creation would equally apply to Berkeley's, as he must have been aware when he wrote that

> . . . many of the wisest of the Ancients, and some of the most enlightened among the Moderns [believe] that the whole Creation was rather an *energy* than a work, by which

the Infinite Being, who is present at all times in all places, exhibits to the minds of his creatures a set of perceptions, like a wonderful picture or piece of musick, always varied, yet always uniform.

In his translation of the Vedantic *Hymn to Narayena*, Jones writes of the 'one only being,'

> Of all perceptions one abundant source
> Whence every object every moment flows.
>   (*Works*. XIII. 302)

Such is the unanimity of tradition that it is not always possible to say with certainty whether Blake, in many of his finest passages, had in mind Berkeley, or the Hermetica, or Vedanta – all in some degree known to him. Vala, his nature-goddess, is the same as Maya, Isis, all the 'veiled' goddesses of antiquity; and Vala's 'veil' of phenomenal appearance is woven by her 'daughters':

> According as they weave the little embryon nerves & veins,
> The Eye, the little Nostrils & the delicate Tongue, & Ears
> Of labyrinthine intricacy, so shall they fold the World,
> That whatever is seen upon the Mundane Shell, the same
> Be seen upon the Fluctuating Earth woven by the Sisters.
>   . . .
> As a beautiful Veil, so there Females shall fold & unfold,
> According to their will, the outside surface of the Earth,
> An outside shadowy Surface superadded to the real Surface
> Which is unchangeable for ever & ever . . .   (K. 728)

The real surface Blake is supposing would be seen if we had 'infinite perception.'

It was Berkeley who broke down the Cartesian distinction between the 'primary' and 'secondary' qualities of objects. Descartes had understood that such things as colour, scent and sound cannot be said to exist without a perceiving mind; but he held time and space to be fixed and eternal. Berkeley defended the Platonic view. 'The soul is its own place,' Plotinus had said; and Berkeley that 'all (place or) extension exists only in the mind' (B. II. 70). In *Siris* he speaks of the Pythagoreans and Platonists who saw that 'there was no such thing as absolute space: that mind, soul or spirit truly and really exists: that bodies exist only in a secondary and dependent sense: that soul is the place of forms' (B. V. 125) – an argument set out at length in the *Hermetica*, and especially in the *Asclepian Dialogue*, where it is argued that the soul is not in the world, but the world in the soul; and in Book X, where the disciple is told to 'Consider him that contains all things, and understand that nothing is more capacious than that which is incorporeal' (*Hermetica*. X. 119)

Berkeley, following these Platonic and Hermetic sources, speaks of 'God' as the incorporeal which contains all things, 'That supreme and wise spirit, *in whom we live, move, and have our being*,' but stops short at the Vedantic affirmation that the mind that creates all sensible things is the human imagination. Blake does take this final step; for him 'Jesus, the Imagination' is the divine presence in man, 'the Divine Humanity,' the Indian *tat tvam asi* – 'that art thou.' 'There is a Throne in every Man, it is the Throne of God,' (K. 661). Blake declares; and 'Around the Throne Heaven is open'd & the Nature of Eternal Things Display'd, All Springing from the Divine Humanity. All beams from him' (K. 612). And again, 'All Things are comprehended in their Eternal Forms in the divine body of the Saviour, the True Vine of Eternity, The Human Imagination, who appear'd to Me as Coming to Judgment among his Saints & throwing off the Temporal that the Eternal might be Established' (K. 605–6). Constantly Blake describes everything in the world as living and as human. It is alive because its existence is in the living mind; and it is human because that perceiving mind is – so far as it is known to us – human. Those bright angelic figures who in Blake's engravings for *The Book of Job* illustrate the words 'The stars of the morning sang together, and all the sons of God shouted for joy': in *The Book of Thel*, the clod of clay, the cloud, and the worm 'on its dewy bed': the 'innumerable company of the heavenly host' who in the sun cry 'Holy, Holy, Holy is the Lord God Almighty'; all these are not personifications of unliving things, but have their life and humanity in mind and thought.

For all things exist in the human imagination.

(K. 707)

The Last Judgment is the realisation that the temporal world is illusory, and times and spaces 'visions' of the living imagination:

> . . . in Visions
> In new Expanses, creating exemplars of Memory and of Intellect,
> Creating space, Creating Time, according to the wonders Divine
> Of Human Imagination . . .
>
> (K. 746)

Such, says Blake, is the variation of time and space 'Which vary according as the Organs of Perception vary' (K. 746). In *Auguries of Innocence* Blake reflects on the 'absolute space' of the Philosopher:

> The Emmet's Inch & Eagle's Mile
> Make Lame Philosophy to smile.
>
> (K. 433)

It must seem at once wild and strangely prosaic to readers of Blake who have not considered how deeply he was involved in the controversy of materialist and immaterialist philosophies that he should say that within 'the Body of Jesus' – who is the Imagination or Ishvara – 'Length, Bredth, Highth again Obey the Divine Vision' (K. 664). He is reaffirming, as against Locke's 'boundless invariable ocean of duration and expansion,' that 'nothing is more capacious than that which is incorporeal.' All spaces and places are in reality created by the one universal imagination which in every individual being varies the ratio at will:

> At will Contracting into Worms or Expanding into Gods,
> . . . tho' we sit down within
> The plowed furrow, list'ning to the weeping clods till we
> Contract or Expand Space at will, or if we raise ourselves
> Upon the chariots of the morning, Contracting or Expanding Time,
> Every one knows we are One Family, One Man blessed for ever.
>
> (K. 686–7)

The one divine mind or Imagination of God is in all, Blake insists; 'Those in Great Eternity,' he wrote in an early poem, *Vala*, are

> As one Man, for contracting their Exalted Senses
> They behold Multitude, or Expanding they behold as one,
> As one Man all the Universal Family . . .

At this point let us return once more to the question of Berkeley's direct influence upon Blake. If a professional philosopher were to take the parallels between these two temperamentally so contrasted thinkers piecemeal it might be argued that Blake by opposing Locke had hit upon the same argument as one used by Berkeley, either through native intelligence, or through participation in the same tradition; by way of Plotinus or the *Hermetica*, or (as perhaps in the passages on animal instinct) from Swedenborg. But as the similarities are seen to multiply this piecemeal dismissal becomes difficult. In *Auguries of Innocence* (written about 1803, shortly before *Milton*) lines 105–10 seem as concise a summary of Berkeley's philosophy as could be made:

> The Emmet's Inch & Eagle's Mile
> Make Lame Philosophy to smile.
> He who Doubts from what he sees
> Will ne'er Believe, do what you Please.
>
> (K. 433)

At about the same time, in *The Mental Traveller*, Blake is describing a cultural reversal and the onset of a materialist phase of civilisation; the 'visionary' Garden of Eden fades, and

> The Guests are scatter'd thro' the land,
> For the Eye altering alters all;
> The Senses roll themselves in fear,
> And the flat Earth becomes a Ball;
>
> (K. 426)

It would I think be difficult to avoid the conclusion that Blake had read Berkeley when he wrote these passages; and in *Milton*, his great refutation of the materialist philosophy, the relativity of time and space is Blake's central theme. One of Berkeley's most original contributions to thought is his argument for the relativity of space and time. Blake, for all his genius for the existential realisation of philosophic ideas in terms of lived experience, was not a philosopher. Nowhere do we find his intuitive perceptions supported by systematic argument; and it seems in every way more likely that Blake has taken Berkeley's conclusions as his starting-point than that he reached so subtle a philosophic realisation unaided.

Whitehead (the philosopher of Einstein's mathematics, as Locke was of Newton's) praised Berkeley for having made the right criticisms of Newton's view of the universe, mentioning in particular his overthrowing of the idea of simple location in space and time. The realities of nature are, according to Whitehead, 'the events of nature' (*Science and the Modern World*, p. 102) and the unit of natural occurrence is what he calls the 'event'. Accordingly, a non-materialistic philosophy of nature will identify a primary organism as being 'the emergence of some particular pattern as grasped in the unity of a real event' (p. 146) and 'Temporalisation (is) the realisation of a complete organism. This organism is an event holding in its essence its spatio-temporal relationships . . . ' Locke had indeed begged the whole question of duration when he defined a 'moment' as his unit of time, 'the time of one *idea* in our Minds, in the train of their ordinary succession there'; 'The hours of folly are measur'd by the clock; but of wisdom, no clock can measure.' So Blake replied in his *Proverbs of Hell*. (K. 151) Berkeley likewise had replied to Locke that since time is nothing, 'abstracted from the succession of ideas in our minds, it follows that the duration of any finite spirit must be estimated by the number of ideas or actions succeeding each other in that same spirit or mind.'

To return to Blake. It is in *Milton* that he attempted fully to set forth existentially what Berkeley had argued discursively – the mental and imaginative nature of time and space. Blake saw that it follows, if times and spaces are created by and in consciousness, that every man – indeed every living creature, 'the little winged fly' or the worm 'translucent all within' – is the creator of its own universe with its times and spaces. In an eloquent passage he defends against Newton's 'globes rolling through voidness' the flat earth of living experience:

The Sky is an immortal Tent built by the Sons of Los:
And every Space that a Man views around his dwelling-place
Standing on his own roof or in his garden on a mount
Of twenty-five cubits in height, such space is his Universe:

(The 'garden on a mount' is Paradise; which every man can see with his own eyes, 'twenty-five cubits' from the ground)

> And on its verge the Sun rises & sets, the Clouds bow
> To meet the flat Earth & Sea in such as order'd Space:
> The Starry heavens reach no further, but here bend and set
> On all sides, & the two Poles turn on their valves of gold;
> And if he move his dwelling-place his heavens also move
> Where'er he goes, & all his neighbourhood bewail his loss.
> Such are the Spaces called Earth & such its dimension.
>
> (K. 516)

It seems clear that Blake had been reading Newton's Principia at this time; for the phrases about the 'moving' of places occur in the following passage:

> As the order of the parts of Time is immutable, so also is the order of the parts of Space. Suppose those parts to be mov'd out of their places, they will be moved (if the expression may be allowed) out of themselves. For time and spaces are, as it were, the Places as well of themselves as of all other things. All things are placed in Time as to order of Succession; and in Space as to order of Situation. It is from their essence or nature that they are Places; and that the primary places of things should be moveable, is absurd. These are therefore the absolute places; and translations out of those places, are the only Absolute Motions . . . *If a place is mov'd, whatever is placed therein moves along with it; and therefore a body, which is mov'd from a place in motion, partakes also of the motion of its place.* (*Mathematical Principles* 1. 12–14)

From these definitions Newton proceeds to define 'immovable space'; and Blake's phrase, 'such its dimension' occurs a few lines below the passage quoted. Blake, with characteristic abruptness, drops from eloquence to prosaic argument; and from Newton he goes on to answer Locke:

> As to that false appearance which appears to the reasoner
> As of a Globe rolling through Voidness, it is a delusion of Ulro.
> The Microscope knows not of this nor the Telescope; they alter
> The ratio of the Spectator's Organs but leave Objects untouched.

In the context not only of Blake's whole work, but also of the foregoing lines, it seems clear that Blake in speaking of the 'object' does not mean Locke's object, situated in 'corporeal space' but Berkeley's object of vision, which is 'untouched' by microscope or telescope, for it does not depend on these in any way, being of a mental nature. Blake continues:

> For every Space larger than a red Globule of Man's blood
> Is visionary, and is created by the Hammer of Los:
> And every space smaller than a Globule of Man's blood opens
> Into Eternity of which this vegetable Earth is but a shadow.

Berkeley, arguing that things 'exist no longer than they are perceived' writes that 'it may to some perhaps seem very incredible, that things should be every moment creating.' To some, perhaps; but not to William Blake, who (again in *Milton*) wrote:

> Los stands creating the glorious sun each morning
> And when unwearied in the evening, he creates the Moon . . .
> (K. 517)

(Blake was an essentially diurnal poet, and only created the moon occasionally, it seems.)

As against the 'moment' of time and 'atom' of space of the scientists, Blake's unit is a unit of life: the 'red globule' of man's blood:

> The red Globule is the unwearied Sun by Los created
> To measure Time and Space to mortal Men every morning.
> (K. 517)

Just as the visible world is created by the 'sons of Los', so are its times:

> But others of the Sons of Los build Moments & Minutes & Hours
> And Days & Months & Years & Ages & Periods, wondrous buildings

Blake's supreme affirmation of the immeasurability of thought concludes with the lines

> Every Time less than a pulsation of the artery
> Is equal in its period & value to Six Thousand Years

(Six thousand years, a figure based on Biblical calculations, was the supposed duration of the earth)

> For in this Period the Poet's Work is Done, & all the Great
> Events of Time start forth & are conceiv'd in such a Period,
> Within a Moment, a Pulsation of the Artery.
>
> (K. 156)

In his poem *Milton* Blake sets forth with an eloquence equalled only by the force of his argument, his vision of this world as it exists in mind and thought. We must live by the imagination; and the world itself will then, and only then, appear to us as it is. Blake is a poet of humanity; but no nature-poet has ever evoked a vision of nature more radiant than Blake does in *Milton* – nature as it appears to the imagination. In the following passage, it is not the physical eye but the living spirit of sight – whom Blake calls Ozoth – who regulates vision:

> The Sons of Ozoth within the Optic Nerve stand fiery glowing,
> And the number of his Sons is eight millions & eight.

(Perhaps the 'eight millions' refers to the population of England at the turn of the eighteenth century; for every human being there is a 'son of Ozoth'.)

> They give delights to the man unknown; artificial riches
> They give to scorn, & their possessors to trouble & sorrow & care,
> Shutting the sun & moon & stars & trees & clouds & waters
> And hills out from the Optic Nerve, & hardening it into a bone
> Opake and like the black pebble on the enraged beach,
> While the poor indignant is like the diamond which, tho' cloth'd
> In rugged covering in the mine, is open all within
> And in his hallow'd center holds the heavens of bright eternity.

> Ozoth here builds walls of rocks against the surging sea,
> And timbers crampt with iron cramps bar in the joys of life
> From fell destruction in the Spectrous cunning & rage. He Creates
> The speckled Newt, the Spider & Beetle, the Rat & Mouse,
> The Badger & Fox: they worship before his feet in trembling fear.
>
> (K. 515)

There are 'sons of Ozoth' also for the animals, for the badger and the fox. It is the living agent of vision that creates the creatures in all their variety, and who opens within man the 'heavens of bright eternity'. Having disposed of Newton's optics by presenting an alternative view of the nature of sight, Blake goes on to demolish time with its endless extension; for time too is created by our experience of it; 'The hours of folly are measur'd by the clock; but of wisdom, no clock can measure.'   (K. 151)

But others of the Sons of Los built Moments & Minutes & Hours
And Days & Months & Years & Ages & Periods, wondrous buildings;
And every Moment has a Couch of gold for soft repose,
(A Moment equals the pulsation of the artery)
And between every two Moments stands a Daughter of Beulah
To feed the Sleepers on their Couches with maternal care.
And every Minute has an azure Tent with silken Veils:
And every Hour has a bright golden Gate carved with skill:
And every Day & Night has Walls of brass & Gates of adamant,
Shining like precious Stones & ornamented with appropriate signs;
And every Month a silver paved Terrace builded high:
And every Year invulnerable Barriers with high Towers:
And every Age is Moated deep with Bridges of silver & gold:
And every Seven Ages is Incircled with a Flaming Fire.
Now Seven Ages is amounting to Two Hundred Years.
Each has its Guard, each Moment, Minute, Hour, Day, Month & Year.

All are the work of Fairy hands of the Four Elements:
The Guard are Angels of Providence on duty evermore.
Every Time less than a pulsation of the artery
Is equal in its period & value to Six Thousand Years.
For in its Period Poet's Work is Done, and all the Great
Events of Time start forth & are conceiv'd in such a Period.
Within a Moment, a Pulsation of the Artery.

(K. 516)

'Six thousand years' is the supposed duration of the time-world, calculated from dates in the Bible. The figure has of course nothing to do with geological time. Time is relative – the universe in itself is timeless. Seen from the standpoint of the timeless spirit 'Time is the mercy of eternity', a space given to fallen mankind in which to discover our true nature and to return to the imaginative knowledge of the infinite and eternal; a condition to which the saints and sages of all religions have testified. Was Yeats remembering the last three lines of this passage when he wrote, in *Leda and the Swan*

> A shudder in the loins engenders there
> The broken wall, the burning roof and tower
> And Agamemnon dead . . .
>
> (Y. 241)

Blake believed not only that the materialist philosophy was mistaken (as did Berkeley) but also that it was the source of great unhappiness, of spiritual sickness in Western civilization, and in England especially. But has he failed in his prophecy – which is also Swedenborg's prophecy, and Yeats's – of a new age based on the traditional teaching common to Berkeley and to Blake that 'Mental Things are alone Real'? (K. 617). The apparent dominance of materialism notwithstanding, it does seem that in this century 'facts of mind' have become the theme not only of those apocalyptic popular movements whose supporters invoke the new 'Age of Aquarius' but of much of the most significant thought. Will the writings of Berkeley and of Blake together with those works which inspired their thought be among the sacred books, perhaps, of an age in which not matter but mind will again be the theme of philosopher and poet; perhaps even of the scientist?

> . . . a voice
> Soft as the rustle of a seed from Cloyne
> That gathers volume; now a thunder-clap.
>
> (Y. 272)